Caldwell on Competitive

Cross-Country Skiing

CALDWELL

ON COMPETITIVE
CROSS-COUNTRY SKIING

John Caldwell

A Greenemont Book

THE STEPHEN GREENE PRESS
BRATTLEBORO, VERMONT

This book has been produced in the United States of America. It is designed by Robert R. Anderson, and published by The Stephen Greene Press, Brattleboro, Vermont 05301.

LIBRARY OF CONGRESS CATALOGING IN PUBLICATION DATA
Caldwell, John H   1928-
    Caldwell on competitive cross-country skiing.
    Edition of 1975 published under title: Caldwell on cross-country training and technique for the serious skier.
    "A Greenemont book."
    Includes index.
    1. Cross-country skiing—Training. I. Title.
GV855.5.T73C34   1979   796.9'3   79-18726
ISBN 0-8289-0359-X
ISBN 0-8289-0360-3 pbk.

Contents

. . . And with My Thanks

First, the illustrations in this book. Photos 4, 13 and 50 are by Tim Caldwell; 8 is by Peter Caldwell; 12, 46, 47 and 48 were executed by Robert R. Anderson from material supplied by Jennifer Caldwell and me; the remaining pictures are mine. I took them with my motor-driven Pentax, and, while they'll not win any photography awards, they do show good training practices or good techniques. You may recognize some of the skiers, since they are among the best in the world. None of them requested or received any remuneration, gift or benefit in return for giving permission to be photographed: The ones who posed did it to help me with this book, and to advance the sport of x-c skiing.

I've always wanted to write about training in conjunction with x-c techniques but when I started this project a number of years ago I got so absorbed in the mass of new material on sports medicine that I started to feel I would have to go to medical school in order to understand better what I was reading, or to be able to test some theories I'd arrived at on my own. Then two physicians who are also excellent athletes—Peter Caldwell and "Skip" Sheldon—came to my rescue. They have been enormously patient in explaining many matters to me. All medically correct information in this book is theirs; any errors are mine.

Over the nearly 30 years that I've been coaching x-c I've worked with a number of women skiers; juniors or seniors, they have my great respect as people and as competitors. However, I find it very awkward to haul up short in my writing and insert *or she/her/hers*. Therefore *he/him/his* are used in the general and classical sense throughout this book, and I hope no one will regard my style as a slur. Certainly none is intended.

Finally, this book is written as a tribute to all the friends—athletes, coaches, doctors, parents and officials—I've made in x-c racing around the world. Females or males, they are called *sportsmen* in every language. All have been friendly and generous in sharing their knowledge with me, and I am grateful.   J.C.

1. A Hard Look at Competition

When I was writing the first edition of this book back in 1974 there still remained in the minds of some a cleavage—artificial, to be sure—between cross-country touring and cross-country ski racing. For touring, some ten years earlier I had coined the word *tourskier*, even though at the time I stressed that the difference from the racer was mainly a matter of degree or intensity of application.

Now, with x-c—cross-country skiing—having grown so much and having started to reach a point which approximates the Scandinavian approach, I can write specifically for the racer without any backing and filling. There are tens of thousands of ardent tourskiers who are enjoying the competition of an increasing number of citizens' races. This interest will in turn help to bring on more youngsters with the ability to train and perfect their technique until many of them can acquit themselves creditably against top racers around the world.

The immediate challenge to our top racers, at this writing, will come in the 1980 Olympics at Lake Placid. Our best skiers know what they are up against but the newly awakened public may not. No doubt the x-c races and all the publicity accruing from them will prove instructive for all of us, and after the Games we will all be further along toward an understanding of x-c competition at every level.

To the individual competitor I say simply this: Your most valid reaction after a race, if you get beaten, is knowing that the fellow who beat you took less time on the course than you did. Don't be looking for a touchstone to his success. Don't suddenly decide to change your training methods, or to adopt a particular ski, or to copy an idiosyncrasy of the winner's technique. Instead, try to evaluate your own performance against your expectation. That's what is important.

Meanwhile . . .

We can all have our own "Olympics," whether it's a local club race, a big citizens' race, or some of the officially sanctioned U.S. and Canadian Ski Association races. The competition is increasing at all levels and this book is addressed to all the skiers who compete.

I hasten to point out the nontechnical aspects of the material that follows. I've read countless journals, reports, books and articles on training. Many

1. Still among Norway's best in 1979: Magne Myrmo (left), coach of the Women's Team, and Oddvar Braa, winner of the first x–c World Cup at the age of 28. Here they pause during a visit to Putney in 1973.

of them are written in technical language I am not thoroughly familiar with, like Medicalese. In writing this I have tried to make it understandable for the average skier, at the same time using or introducing some terms that I find necessary to use, or terms which will help to raise the general level of knowledge about the subject. However, there are not a lot of highfalutin explanations to go along with many of the statements I make, although I know this poses a danger because some may find it easy to poke holes in what is written.

I'm not going to list any references either. I've read three-page listings of references that accompany two-page reports and I want to avoid anything like that. It's time-consuming and takes a lot of space. Besides, I have not taken much material from any particular source. Most of it is common knowledge to many coaches around the world, but even more of it has derived from my continuous years of coaching since 1951. I've tried here to bring across material that will help parents, friends and coaches of racers of any age.

Even if you don't ski yourself you could find plenty that will aid in helping others. If reading this book encourages anyone interested in the sport to enjoy any part of the x-c scene I will feel I have put something into a program which means so much to me.

How Far, How Early?

During the last few years the United States has been putting a great deal of emphasis on junior development in x-c ski racing. The usual approach heard is that the juniors are our main hope in international competition, that we must broaden the base, we need a farm system, and so on. The U.S. Ski Team, Inc., has managed to corral large sums of money for a development program.

It may be that we have felt the pressure from some of the Eastern Bloc countries, notably East Germany, where they start programming kids in their early 'teens, or before. So we have young teams, development teams, younger junior teams, Baby Blue teams, and the like. The kids are showered with attention in the form of free equipment, plane tickets, invitations to training camps, and special coaching from the national staff.

It may be too early to see the results of this approach but so far I tend to be skeptical about it. I favor a much more conservative policy that keeps the kids at home under local guidance as much as possible, so they can feel support from their home area first of all. They need to learn or develop a love for the sport that is natural, or a way of life.

For Coaches: Do It Too

I've been involved in just about every facet of cross-country skiing since the early 1940's and I occasionally look back on them to judge their value to me as a coach. I would say that now I learn more, or get more ideas, from training and racing myself than from any other activity. By training I can experience many of the feelings the athletes do when they train. These aren't restricted to daily feelings, but include things like peaking for big races. And by racing I get the best possible chance to try wax combinations, different pacing routines, and even different techniques.

So many times we coaches stand on the sidelines and give assurances to our racers about the wax, or we tell them how they should ski a certain hill, and so on. But I can tell you there is nothing like the acid test. I recommend that all you coaches go through at least a couple of weeks' training with your skiers and that you enter a few races every year. Chances are good that you'll learn something; and you'll probably enjoy yourself as well.

If some of our *Wunderkinder* of today are shut off from their free equipment and plane tickets, these more material things, I wonder if we will not have taken away a big source of their incentive. Then what happens? They quit before they reach their early twenties when they might be able to show significant results, and we have lost a rather big investment, so to speak. On the other hand, if the juniors are brought along more gradually and allowed to develop on the local level they may feel more allegiance toward the sport; and if they do, it will surely come at an important time in their development.

Cross-country skiing is not like gymnastics or swimming, where top competitors are in their 'teens. Rather, the history of x-c is filled with wonderful feats by some of the "old-timers." Oddvar Braa won the first World Cup title at the ripe old age of twenty-eight. He had some good results in earlier years but nothing to compare with those during his 1979 season. And during that same season, Galina Kulakova, aged thirty-eight, climbed out of her wheelchair and won the World Cup for women. That older x-c skiers do well comes as no surprise to most students of the sport, which historically utilizes maturity. There is a lot to learn and reaching the top often takes years of emotional training, to say nothing of physical training. I believe that the best way to broaden the base in North America is to encourage x-c as a family, or club, or community activity, as the Europeans do.

One more example: The present Finnish training program is geared so that an athlete reaches his heaviest training in sheer load when he is twenty-three or twenty-four years old. The implication is obvious. The Finns are content to bring their skiers along slowly until then and see what happens afterward.

Fortunately, the sport is growing fast in North America and there are increased local or regional opportunities for more skiers who are in their twenties. The competition is getting stiffer—a fact which actually seems to be having a salutary effect on this age group, for whatever reason.

2. Coaches' & Athletes' Language

Lots of coaches and skiers apparently have disagreements on many points when they talk about training. After careful investigation, though, it turns out that the parties really just have different definitions in mind when making certain statements, and so there are actually fewer conflicts of opinion than seem to exist. Let's eliminate a part of this language barrier by agreeing now on working definitions for many of the terms that crop up later in this book.

Metric system

I use the metric system throughout this book because all ski distances are measured in kilometers and all the scientific literature uses liters, milliliters, etc.

For the uninitiated, a kilometer is about 6/10 mile and a liter is a little more than one U.S. liquid quart, so watch out when they serve you a liter of beer abroad or you'll get loop-legged in about half the time.

Here are some lengths:

1 centimeter (cm) = .3937 inch (about 4/10 inch); *1 meter (m)* = 100 cm = 39.37 inches (about 1 1/12 yards); *1 kilometer (km)* = .62137 mile (about 6/10 mile); *5 km* = about 3 miles; *10 km* = about 6 miles; *15 km* = about 9 miles; *30 km* = about 19 miles; *50 km* = about 31 miles.

The standard ski-racing distances are 5, 10, 15, 30 and 50 km. It's interesting to note that track people run races of 5,000 m or 10,000 m, while skiers refer to these same distances as 5 k's or 10 k's.

Here are some volume measures (liquid):

1 milliliter (ml) = 1.000027 cubic centimeters (cc) = .061025 cubic inch = .0338147 U.S. fluid ounce.

1 liter (l) = 1000 ml = 1000.027 cc = 61.025 cu in = 33.8147 U.S. fluid oz = about 1.06 U.S. quarts.

And it takes 453.5924 *grams* to make 1 pound, or about 28 grams to tip an ounce on a balance.

2. Early spring, following several weeks' layoff after the racing season, is the time to ease into training routine again. These skiers are taking hikes with poles through the Vermont woods, where there are as yet no leaves to hide views of new routes.

Physiological terms

Oxygen-transport System

This includes all those processes by which oxygen is inspired and delivered to the tissues. An important part of this transport system is the heart and circulating blood. A simple equation will explain further:

$$\frac{ml\ blood\ pumped}{min} = \frac{heart\ beats}{min} \times \frac{ml\ blood\ pumped}{beat}$$

12

Or, translated from the Algebra:

$$Cardiac\ output = Heart\ rate \times Stroke\ volume$$

Training increases the stroke volume, which in turn permits maintenance of any given cardiac output at a reduced heart rate. This is important because the perfusion of heart muscle occurs during the relaxation phase of the cardiac cycle. Thus, with a slower heart rate there is more time for adequate blood perfusion of the heart muscle.

Training works in other ways to augment the oxygen-transport system. Consider:

$$\frac{ml\ O_2}{min} = \frac{ml\ blood}{min} \times \frac{ml\ O_2}{ml\ blood}$$

Or:

$$Oxygen\ transport = Cardiac\ output \times Oxygen\ content\ of\ blood$$

3. Jennifer Caldwell is expert at using a splitting wedge for the family's winter woodpile—after her brothers fell and buck up the trees.

4. Mike Gallagher, Bob Gray and Mike Elliott (left to right) sparked U.S. Teams from 1962 to 1974 in the Olympics and all major FIS competitions. Their dedication to the sport made the world's ski powers begin to take America's x-c efforts seriously.

Training increases the red-cell mass of the circulating blood volume, thereby increasing the capacity of oxygen in any given volume of blood. This is important because any given level of oxygen transport can be achieved at a reduced cardiac output.

Red Blood Cells

These are erythrocytes to the medical profession, and are often abbreviated "RBC" in articles and books. In a normal human adult there are about five million RBC per cubic millimeter.

RBC's are the cells that carry hemoglobin, the O_2-carrying protein. The hemoglobin content is often expressed in grams per hundred milliliters of whole blood; thus a hemoglobin count of 15 percent—which is regarded as normal for healthy adults—means 15 grams per one hundred ml of blood.

Mitochondria

These are the parts of normal cells where the reactions take place which produce high-energy compounds necessary for muscle contractions.

Oxygen-utilization System

This involves the total cumulative metabolic processes in the tissues requiring oxygen. At present there is some evidence that these chemical processes may be facilitated as a result of training.

Oxygen Uptake (VO₂)

This is the oxygen utilized per unit-time (usually one minute), and may be limited by the oxygen transport and oxygen utilization systems described above. Hence, oxygen uptake is influenced by training. Indeed, many physiologists believe the measurements of maximal oxygen uptake to be the best index of physical fitness.

If one person has a maximum oxygen uptake (max O_2 uptake) of 6 liters (6 l) per minute, and another person has a max uptake of 3 l per minute, I think you can see what will happen if both engage in an exercise like running which might require 3 l per minute in this case. The first person will be cruising along, working at 50 percent of his capacity while the second person will be working at 100 percent, or all out. And soon the second fellow will be all out—of gas.

Oxygen Debt

Oxygen debt might be expected to occur when oxygen utilization exceeds oxygen uptake for any appreciable length of time.

Only small amounts of oxygen are present in solution in the tissues; the rest is in the lungs (as air) and in the blood. There is little change in the oxygen content of the respiratory system (lungs and blood) during exercise. Further, the volume of oxygen stores (1650 ml or about 3½ liquid pints) is almost insignificant when one considers that it represents only about 15 seconds' worth of the max O_2 uptake of a person who has a capacity for 6 liters per minute.

Steady-state Condition

Essentially all the work done in a strenuous endurance event such as an x-c ski race is performed during a steady-state condition where there is a balance between the oxygen consumed by the tissues and the oxygen delivered or transported to the tissues. It's so important that I'll say it again: Training increases the capacity of the cardiorespiratory system for O_2 transport, so the more O_2 you can deliver the more you have available for consumption and the faster you can go.

Aerobic/Anaerobic

Aerobic work is a general—and therefore imprecise—term that is used to designate effort expended under steady-state conditions with respect to oxygen.

Anaerobic work, on the other hand, is that effort which is expended under conditions of presumed oxygen debt, such as a sprint event like the 100-meter dash.

Glycogen/Glucose

This is the storage form of carbohydrate; readily mobilized as glucose, it is used as a source of energy during exercise. There is some evidence that training and diet may increase glycogen stores in the liver and muscles. (See Chapter 11, on diet.)

5. Bill Koch's year-round cardiovascular training sure paid off in the 1976 Olympics. (This shot, taken in 1972, shows that his distinctive style was already developed.)

Fatty Acids

Fatty acids are the other important source of energy during exercise, and some experiments in animals suggest these may be preferable to glucose in sustained exercise to the limits of endurance.

Lactate

Lactate (lactic acid) is an intermediate in the chemical degradation of glucose to carbon dioxide and water. Trained athletes maintain lower levels of circulating lactate during exercise than untrained athletes. This suggests that training may facilitate the metabolism of lactate.

It is thought that the disagreeable sensations (such as numbness) sometimes occurring in extreme effort may be in part accounted for by an increased level of circulating lactate in the acid form.

Coaches' terms

Going Under

This term is deliberately descriptive, rather than precise. It refers to the sensations of numbness, clumsiness, stiffness, muscle pain, blurred vision, paresthesia, dizziness, and imminent collapse which come at the limit of effort.

The causes for these symptoms are very likely to be multiple, and may include lack of oxygen, abundant lactic acid, and other circulating metabolites as yet unidentified.

Hyperventilation

Hyperventilating is a breathing technique wherein a person takes in more oxygen than he normally would under the circumstances; actually, it's force-feeding with oxygen. There may be some argument as to the value of hyperventilating, but it certainly serves to alert and relax an athlete—especially when done before going up a long hill—and this in itself is worthwhile.

Peaking

Peaking, or being "at peak," is that condition when an athlete is producing his optimum results. The skiers who finish back in the pack also peak, just like the winners, but unfortunately not so much is made of it. This does not detract from the value of peaking, or the knowledge that a skier has peaked.

Often, after seeing a skier's best results, we nod our heads sagely and declare that he has peaked. "At peak" means a racer *is* ready to, or actually *is performing* at his top level (there's more of this in Chapter 10). The real challenge is to be able to predict peaks, not comment on them after the fact.

Upper Limit/Limiting Factor

Coaches and physiologists talk about the upper limits of exercise for an individual, meaning as far as he can go, or as intensely as he can work. Some also talk about limiting factors.

For example: "The O_2 utilization system may be the limiting factor in exercise." This means that theoretically an athlete could do more work if he could just utilize more oxygen—the O_2 is there, the lungs can take it in, absorb it, the heart can pump it to the muscles, but the chemical processes aren't efficient enough to utilize all the O_2.

Well, at best this is a gray area. Many of the top physiologists will not agree on what the limiting factors are in exercise, or if there are any at all. Some say that all the factors converge to a limit, others feel that one hundred years from now athletes may be able to run 1500 meters at a rate close to the present rate for 100 meters.

During the past five years there has been a revival of interest in training physiology in the U.S.A. Many topics are under active investigation, including the analysis of the effects of exercise on muscle glycogen stores, testing for optimal food-energy sources in exercise, investigation of intracellular oxygen transport, and so on. Coaches and athletes alike will be only too eager to explore any new leads which may develop from these studies.

Optimum

Webster is the best authority here: "The best or most favorable degree, quantity, number, etc."

Nice word. If you race for a distance at your optimum rate it is usually taken to mean that you have gone just as fast as you could; and this in turn means you have done it under steady-state conditions of oxygen supply and demand for the major part of the time.

If you train at your optimum rate you are going at the rate which is most efficient in terms of conditioning. Naturally there is some controversy about the optimum rate of training. Some will say it's 50 percent of maximum O_2 uptake; others think training, at least much of it, should be at 100 percent of maximum; and then there are lots of in-between theories. I'll go into this in a separate section.

Warm-up

I mean "warm" in the literal sense. My standard warm-up is accomplished by running or skiing easily with plenty of clothing on. After I'm warmed I usually feel just a little more alive—you know, I can count my pulse in more places, I begin to perspire gently and, at the same time, actually feel relaxed—then, after that, I stretch occasionally.

6. Tim Caldwell of the U.S. Team at the end of a 3-km sprint uphill on roller skis during a summer training session in 1973, some 18 months after his first Olympics, in Sapporo.

You too should always be warmed up before you try any vigorous stretching exercises.

There are all sorts of other warm-ups that involve calisthenics and the like. These are fine but they border on what I term a workout.

It's well accepted that your body will function better after it is warmed, and therefore a warm-up before racing is a must. On the other hand, many people like to incorporate their warm-ups into their workouts. This is easily done and perfectly acceptable.

Warm-down

After a vigorous workout a warm-down is in order. This should be a relaxed, cooling-off period, and could be done in the same way you did

7. This could be logged under "interval training": an early fall hill-climbing workout pauses—just by chance, of course—in Bill Darrow's apple orchard.

your warm-up. Recently, stretching exercises have become very popular, and many athletes spend 20–30 minutes at them.

Whatever you do, don't come in from a workout under a full head of steam and then just sit down or go inside and rest. Rather, walk around, or ski easily. Cool off. Flex yourself a bit to see how you feel—and then go in before you get chilled.

Distance Training

This refers to a long workout, done under steady-state conditions, where the distance covered is the dominant feature. A 150-km bike ride is a distance workout, as is a run on foot of 15 km.

Endurance Training

All distance workouts provide endurance training for the cardiovascular system. Long bouts of physical work could be considered endurance training for strength. Weight training that stresses many repetitions, even though the time involved is not as great as that of a distance workout or an eight-hour working effort, is also considered endurance training for strength.

Weight or Strength Training

This is any work or exercise that involves resistance, and thus causes great tension in the muscles being used.

Examples are weight-lifting, pulling elastic armbands, doing hard physical labor like logging, digging ditches, etc.

Isometrics/Isotonics

Isometrics is a contraction of the muscles without movement of the limbs or parts of the body involved. Stand in a doorway and push outward against the sides. If the doorway doesn't collapse you are doing an isometric contraction. I will dispose of isometrics here by stating that I do not think they have any part in a good x-c training program.

Isotonics is a contraction of the muscles that involves movement of the participating limbs and muscles. Weight-lifting is an example.

Interval Training

This is a term used broadly to mean any exercise or activity—but usually running—that is interspersed with periods of less intense activity. There are obvious variables in interval training: the intensity of the activity, the length of the activity, the number of repetitions of the activity, the length of the recovery period (or the less-intense activity period) and its intensity.

A standard interval workout might be running 60-second quarters and jogging 120-second quarters after each; repeat ten times.

Or a person might run natural intervals on a ski trail, putting out extra effort on the uphill sections only, and going easier on the downhills and flats. This type of workout is not as regimented as the track workout but is probably more valuable as x-c ski training.

Tempo/Speed

Tempo training in this book will mean going at a pace equal to racing speed.

It is sometimes confused with *speed training*, which, in this book, means going all out. Speed training, if continued long enough, will cause you to go under.

Specificity

This refers to training or exercises directly connected with the movements required by your event. For instance, roller-skiing and pulling on armbands are both specificity exercises for x-c skiing (see Chapter 7). Almost all weight-lifting is not.

Deconditioning Effect

This is just what it sounds like: a decreasing of the physical condition of the body. It is the generally accepted theory that all training effects are reversible. Some physiologists put it this way: If you train for five years it will take you about five years to decondition, assuming you don't train during that time.

A certain amount of deconditioning can occur during sickness, and some doctors claim that too much bed rest during the competitive season may also cause some deconditioning.

Further, if you set yourself a training schedule that is not progressive you may suffer from deconditioning. This is a very interesting point and I want to dwell on it.

Suppose your goal in training is to be able to run a 7-minute mile three times a week. You begin by jogging, walking, running when you feel comfortable, and you progress slowly. You are conditioning yourself during this period because your level of intensity is increasing during this time. Finally, you reach your goal and can run the mile in 7 minutes.

But you continue at this level. And what happens now is that you get more and more efficient at running the mile and therefore you begin to do less work. Clearly, you won't completely decondition yourself if you maintain this level, but you may eventually come down a bit from your peak at the point of being able to run the 7-minute mile.

In order to continue a progressive training program in this instance you would have a choice between two obvious options: either run the mile faster, or run more than a mile at the same rate. (You could also run the mile with a weighted vest, or run a mile up a gradual incline—the point is to require greater effort.)

Rest Day

This can mean any sort of day that is more restful than those when you train regularly. For some it might be curling up with a book all day, for others some mild exercise. The hotshots talk about active rest days, and for them this might mean going out and running a mere 15 km.

3. The Basis for Training

I have tried to include in this book the gist of what I've learned over nearly thirty years of coaching for x-c competition. There's also a lot of worthwhile information available in other material that ranges from introductions for beginners to highly technical points for experts. And I want to tell you something important about all of it.

First, read it carefully, take it in slowly, leave it alone for a while, and then come back to it.

Next, be skeptical. If you don't like the sound of something, start off with another tack. Proceed with your own thinking on the matter to see where it ends up. I have arrived at several of my own principles or conjectures by doing just that.

Finally, try to reach a point in your own development where you have nearly complete confidence in your own methods, whether you are a racer, a coach, or someone who is primarily training for training's own sake. Don't be too easily influenced by methods that are foreign to you, or by methods that have not worked well for you. Each individual is special. Each behaves and reacts differently. Each can reach his goals by slightly different means.

If you understand this, and can apply it, you will be successful.

But a warning to heed

No matter what your age, you should have a thorough medical examination before you begin any intensive training program. The doctor should be able to tell you of the need for any restrictions.

If you are young and in average health there are probably very few restrictions you have to worry about. Some physiologists believe that healthy people in their teens, or younger, cannot harm themselves by hard training. Their theory is that when a person gets into an extreme exercise stress situation he will simply slow up, naturally or otherwise. I generally agree; but I do warn against competitive situations where young people might be spurred beyond acceptable limits by crowd stimulus, or by a desire to satisfy the emotional parents who might be on the scene, etc.

I remember a theory prevalent several years ago which held that one's growth could be stunted by hard exercise during the formative 'teens. Today the belief is quite the opposite. And many physiologists think that an athlete will develop his oxygen uptake the most, or completely, before the age of 20.

If you are middle-aged (and I'm not going to try and pin *that* one down) and have been used to an active life with a fair amount of exercise, and if you are normally healthy, you can undertake quite a program. In fact, the limiting factors might be your own time and interest. But get a medical check and keep doing so regularly.

People with some form of heart disease should not attempt anything described in this book. Doctors are turning to certain kinds of exercise as rehabilitation in many cases of heart disease, but physicians are the only ones to make such prescriptions.

Where it started

I've dubbed the over-all approach to training as described in this book the Putney Method not to be vainglorious but merely because the concepts were jelled and implemented here in this small hill town in Windham County, Vermont.

The system didn't just show up on the scene: It has evolved over a long period of time. Every good skier who has been connected with Putney in any way has had a hand in the formulation of this system. And the system is changing all the time, too.

A few skiers and coaches I know have taken out of context some of the Putney approaches to training, or have failed to understand them. Perhaps to an outsider who doesn't see how they mesh, they do look a bit loose and discombobulated. So it might be easy to get the impression either that the training methods are not vigorous or that we are keeping secrets from everyone.

But of course we have no secrets. For instance, we in Putney were primarily responsible for introducing hiking, biking, dancing, rowing and roller-skiing into the training programs used by many people. I can recount with amusement the hurdles I had to overcome to convince many coaches of the value of these types of training, because their repertory for several years consisted of running and perhaps a few other exercises like calisthenics.

What are the keys to the program? I would say hard work and intelligent training. Sounds simple and maybe it is. Hard work and intelligent training must come from the athlete's love for the sport, which naturally includes training for it. Cross-country skiing and training is a year-round matter: it's all one. And the more you like to train the harder you will train. So it

8. Some of the locals ready for a workout in Putney. From left: Mike Fairchild, Bill Koch, Katie Tobey Koch, John Caldwell, Tim Caldwell, Jim Galanes, Stan Dunklee.

seems sensible to make training enjoyable and challenging, and I have always had that as my primary goal.

Next, we try to make training as specific as possible—but not to the extent that we lose variety. For instance, an athlete doing hill-bounding and roller-skiing during the entire offseason would be doing specificity exercises but he might soon tire of this regime. So every once in a while he should substitute something else—rowing, hiking, biking, running through the woods, skill games like tennis, volleyball—you name it.

There's something else going for x-c in the Putney area and many recognize it as atmosphere or acceptance. The local people are sympathetic to training, they accept the notions and ideas, they don't nearly drive off the road when they see someone roller-skiing, and so on. These are plus points. Also, the geography of the area lends itself to training, for the terrain and the weather are both conducive to good training.

So perhaps at Putney we've been lucky in these aspects. Now there is a fairly strong tradition in the community and it serves for the betterment of all competitors. At the 1979 National Championships, the Putney Ski Club's men won the three medals in the 15-, 30- and 50-km races, as well as the gold medal in the relay. This is noteworthy in any case, but especially so considering that the club boasts only some 70 members.

Introducing the Caldwell Principles

You will find statements called Caldwell's Principles of Training (CPT) and Caldwell's Principles of Technique (CPTK) sprinkled throughout. Some of these are stated in a way that may seem funny to you; some are funny to me. But at the same time I am perfectly serious about them; they underlie my philosophy of training. Without further ado I introduce my first Principle of Training:

CPT 1: If you read far enough in the sports literature, or talk to enough athletes, trainers and coaches, you can find justification for any number of seemingly conflicting training methods.

A few years ago, for example, word came out that the Germans were putting a great deal of emphasis on interval training and felt it was the best method for building endurance in an athlete. This news roused several coaches and athletes who had been using LSD (please, in track parlance that's short for the Long, Slow, Distance method of training) and they came out with articles and comments citing the advantages of their methods.

Well, the controversy rages on and I hope it's never settled. Wouldn't it be awful if it was conclusively proved that Method X was the best for developing endurance in an athlete? Then everyone would start to train the same way and there would be nothing to speculate about, little more to write and argue about, and much of the interest and variety would be taken out of training.

Another example, easy to understand, comes from the weight-lifting crowd. In order to develop optimum muscular strength some of them prescribe lifting very heavy loads for a maximum of three times (if you can lift it more than three times it's not heavy enough, they say). Others shake their heads in disbelief at this approach and tell us we should use three sets of ten lifts each, with much lighter loads. And so on.

Controversy is fine, it's interesting, and it will continue. The danger for the athlete, as I have observed, is this: Too often skiers will get hold of the past season's star performer and inquire about his training methods. Then, after being told, they will exclaim—"Aha! No wonder we were getting whipped. So-and-so used many more short intervals in early November than we did! That explains it!"

Actually, of course, it doesn't explain anything. You have to set up your own program and gain confidence in it. I know this can be difficult, especially with all the literature coming out on training. (I doubt a person could keep up with this reading even if he had it all at his disposal, in his native tongue—it's being produced that fast.) For every champion endurance-event athlete who stresses one particular system of training, another can be found who stresses an *apparently* conflicting method. So don't be psyched out by someone else's program. Remember CPT 1.

Which leads me to make one more observation and I introduce it by way of CPT 2:

CPT 2: Athletes tend to train hardest using methods or activities in which they are very successful, or which they enjoy most.

For instance, Skier A, who is a good road-runner, will tend to do the largest part of his offseason training by running, entering summer road races, etc. He will justify this by saying that running is the best training and this will be backed up by CPT 1.

Skier B, who loves manual labor—throwing logs around, digging ditches, and so on—will spend most of his training time doing this sort of thing. Easily he can cite strength as being important, and, in passing, hint at the good cardiovascular endurance he is gaining by working hard.

However, it is too often the case that A probably needs more muscle-building work and B needs more running. Therefore the corollary to CPT 2 is this: In *training*, athletes should work on their *weaknesses;* in *competitive events* they should concentrate on their *strengths.*

To give examples which will be obvious: A skier who has very good technique doesn't have to spend his offseason doing a lot of co-ordination training such as trampolining, tumbling, diving and skill games. He probably needs some good distance work. He should concentrate on distance.

And during an x-c race, a skier who is very strong on the uphills yet can't ski too well downhill, should really go all out on the uphill sections. Make time here. On the downhill he should take it easy; check rather than take a chance on falling and losing time.

The Training Effects

Suppose two people who are alike in all their physical characteristics begin a training program. One walks a mile every day in 20 minutes and the other runs a mile every day in 7 minutes. What changes will take place?

To begin with, if these two maintain the same diets there will be little difference in their weight changes due to exercise. That's because each will expend approximately the same amount of energy in doing the mile.

However, the person who is doing the more intense exercise by running the mile will begin to show the effects of training, and if we could measure all these effects after a period of time we would probably find at least the following changes: His rested pulse rate would go down, his cardiac output would increase, his oxygen uptake would increase, and perhaps his ability to utilize oxygen would increase.

It's very important to know what training causes these changes, the so-called training effects, to take place. It isn't so important for us to know why they take place. But a few words on these training effects will be helpful.

O₂ uptake

The oxygen uptake of a person (often expressed as VO_2 in the literature) is the amount of oxygen he utilizes during a certain period of time. Uptake may not be the best word for this process, but it's the one everyone uses. Actually, a person breathes in and absorbs more oxygen into his bloodstream than he utilizes in the production of energy; therefore it's only the oxygen that is utilized for energy that is defined as the measure of a person's uptake.

To determine their oxygen uptake, thousands of people have been tested while exercising vigorously. The testing method is easy to understand but it does require some equipment that you don't find lying around everywhere.

A person runs on a treadmill or pedals on a bicycle ergometer until he reaches the steady state. Then the air that is expired from the lungs is captured in a device called a Douglas Bag, and is compared with the surrounding air (from which he inspired) for the difference in O₂ content. That difference is the O₂ used by the body, or O₂ uptake.

If the intensity of the exercise is increased until the person has to stop from exhaustion, a good measure of his max O₂ uptake can be determined.

Measurements for max O₂ uptake are given in two different ways. You might read that a person's max O₂ uptake is 6 l/min, meaning that he can utilize 6 liters of oxygen per minute. In the section of definitions I compared two people, one with an uptake of 6 l and another with an uptake of 3 l. Imagine what would happen if both were engaged in exercise that required more than 3 l/min. The person with the lower uptake would be forced to stop very soon, and from his example is learned the advantage of having a high O₂ uptake.

You might expect a person weighing 80 kg to use more oxygen to carry himself around than one who weighed 40 kg. And you'd usually be right. Thus, the measurement of O₂ uptake in terms of liters alone is not as meaningful as another system of measurement—one that expresses O_2 uptake in terms of milliliters per kilogram body weight per minute. An athlete's uptake might be expressed as 65 ml/kg, meaning that he can utilize 65 milliliters of O_2 per kilogram of weight per minute. With this measurement we might find that our 40-kg person mentioned above had a higher uptake rate than the one who weighed 80. From there we could be led to assume that the lighter person had a higher capacity for endurance work.

All max O_2 measurements are for the exercise being performed—that is, usually biking or running on a treadmill. Since measuring uptake during skiing or roller-skiing presents certain practical difficulties, there have not been many experiments with skiers. However, a few physiologists, notably some Swedes, have hitched up the gear to skiers and have driven along beside them with the rest of the measuring equipment in order to get some uptake readings.

In general the results show uptakes for skiing as high or higher than those for running and biking. This is not surprising, since skiing uses more muscle-mass than most activities.

Measurements of O_2 uptake can be significant if they are done on the same subject under exactly the same conditions over a period of time, thus allowing progress to be charted. If a batch of skiers is tested for O_2 uptake on the bicycle ergometer, then relative measurements can be determined for that exercise. The correlation between O_2 uptake for biking—the ergometer—and for skiing would be expected to be high. However, there's more to being a successful skier than having a high O_2 uptake. There are little items like strength, technique, motivation and intelligence. The champions on the Douglas Bag don't always show at the top of the results list, so let's not "run our races in the laboratory."

Some Socialist countries test their youngsters at an early age for max O_2 uptake and the quality of muscle fibers, etc., and then program them for particular events. A kid with a high uptake might be encouraged to go into distance events, for instance.

This approach is tied in with a certain theory—or perhaps it's a conjecture at this point. And it is this: that athletes are born with sprint/ strength muscles or with endurance muscles. If you happen to have endurance muscles it means that the muscles' cells are more suited for utilizing O_2 by those chemical processes that take place during exercise, and therefore your uptake would be above normal. In other words, O_2 uptake, to a degree, is inherited. I don't know about this. If O_2 uptake is inherited it ought to be possible to predict an athlete's uptake by measuring his parents and I haven't heard of any experiments along this line.

Science and test scores

As we get more scientific about our training for x-c skiing we must at the same time caution ourselves not to become too dependent on medical tests, scores, and the like. I've seen treadmill and ergometer scores, results of tests for body fat, arm strength, leg strength, etc. All these make for good conversation and they are certainly an indication of potential. But don't read too much into these scores. The doctors are the first ones to warn against this.

One of the first things you should ask yourself about an experiment or a test score is this: What are the variables? Consider a bicycle ergometer test used to determine a person's O_2 uptake. If everything else was equal (and it never is) wouldn't you expect a person who had biked extensively to score higher on this test than someone who had not biked at all? The veteran biker would be more efficient and could therefore carry a heavier load—this would mean a higher score. However, his actual O_2 uptake might be lower than the other fellow's.

Compensation

It has been established that women have average max O_2 uptakes of about 15 percent less than men. (At the same time, a few highly trained women athletes have max O_2 uptakes only 10 percent below those obtained in comparably trained men.) It's very important for women to realize this and accept it. If they try to train, ski, and race on an equal basis with men, they are going to have a very discouraging time of it. However, the enjoyment and the inspiration to be derived from women and men training together should not be underestimated. Many of the world's top skiers of both sexes, and plenty of the tour-racers, take their workouts together to the benefit of everyone.

Suppose it becomes possible to take care of these variables (such as experience in biking) by plugging certain factors into some formula. What then? Couldn't we do a pretty good job of predicting race outcomes? Well, you still must consider other variables in a race situation. How about motivation, technique, ability to pace, good wax, the breaks that often occur during a race, and so on? These will always be variables and no one will ever be able to predict results in good competition by looking at the test scores. Isn't it a lucky thing, too? There wouldn't be any point in having a race if we could figure out the winners in the laboratory beforehand.

But enough of this heavy stuff. Let's be sure we know what training increases your O_2 uptake, a matter that is important for endurance events like x-c skiing.

Cardiac output

The more blood your heart can pump through your body to the working muscles, bringing a fresh supply of oxygen, the more work you will be able to do. As you might expect, there is a high correlation between cardiac output and O_2 uptake.

Tests have shown that during vigorous exercise the maximum pulse rate of a well-trained athlete and an untrained person is about the same. But there is an important difference in the two heart-stroke volumes. The athlete may be able to deliver as much as 40 l of blood per minute whereas the untrained person may deliver only 20 l. In other words, with each stroke or beat of his heart the athlete is pumping twice as much blood. Proper training will increase your stroke volume and this is another of the training effects.

The reason people with low pulse rates are often good bets for endurance events is this: Let's assume two people who are nearly alike in body weight, make-up, etc., are sitting around and we check their pulses. One is 40 a minute and the other is 80. It isn't stretching it too far to assume that the demands for blood are the same in each person and therefore the fellow with the low rate is pumping twice as much blood per stroke. More than this, his heart has twice as long to fill with blood before it is pumped out. This implies a bigger and stronger heart.

But having a good heart that can really pump blood isn't the end-all either. The blood has to get to the working muscles, and for this it is necessary that the muscles relax. Try carrying a bucket full of maple sap up a hill with one arm. Soon your arm gets that numb feeling because the arm muscles are not relaxing and permitting a free flow of blood (this is probably due to a build-up of lactate in your arm). Anyway, what do you do? You stop and rest, or switch arms. In other words, you relax the muscles, fresh blood comes into the numbed arm with a new supply of O_2, and at the same time the blood helps to carry off the lactate.

So it is with skiing. If your technique does not allow your muscles to relax sufficiently the blood will begin to bypass those areas that are constricted—the very areas where you need continuing supplies of blood (and therefore oxygen). In this case it doesn't matter what your cardiac output or your max O_2 uptake is. What does matter is your technique.

Pulse Rate

In general there is a correlation between a person's heart rate, his O_2 uptake at that time, and his cardiac output. This means that the faster your heart beats, within certain limits, the more blood and oxygen you will deliver to your muscles.

It is also generally true that during intense exercise a person's O_2 uptake reaches a maximum, or levels off, before his heart rate reaches a maximum. For instance, if your max heart rate is 200, you might reach your max O_2 uptake at 180 beats. After this point an increased heart rate would not deliver any more oxygen (blood) to the system.

This leads us toward trying to determine the optimum intensity of exercise, or training. Most physiologists and coaches around the world think that an athlete should work very often at his max O_2 uptake. One reason given to support this notion is the belief that the body adjusts to stress situations, and therefore if you train hard your body will learn to function better at these high levels.

If we agree to this theory of training at max O_2 uptakes quite often, the next question is: How do you know when you are at max uptake? First, we can say that it is not when your pulse rates are at maximum. Next, it's probably safe to say that if your max uptake occurs at 180 beats per minute, a rate slightly lower than this will be associated with an O_2 uptake which is 85–90 percent of your max uptake; so this isn't bad.

But there still remains the problem of how to determine this max O_2 uptake intensity, or an optimum intensity for training, and then how to pinpoint when you are working at this rate. If there is anyone in the crowd who can claim to know definitely, will he please step forward?

9. Mike Elliott's splendid conditioning allowed him to train at high-energy output for 20 to 30 km a crack, gave him a strikingly low pulse rate in the low 30's.

How Hard?

There have been attempts to specify an optimum average heart rate for distance workouts. I'll throw out a couple of examples for you, but I cannot recommend only one method over the others with any finality. However, they might serve as a guide.

Try This

One method for determining your *optimum average* heart rate for a distance workout is to multiply your rested pulse by 2½. For me that might be too fast: my rested pulse is about 60 and the formula indicates I should average 150 beats per minute during a distance workout. I don't think I could do it, and that may be because I'm too old.

I know some skiers with rested pulse rates of 40 and if they followed this formula they would work out at 100—hardly worth the effort!

If you are somewhere between these two extremes the 2½ factor might work.

Or This

Perhaps the simplest method is to run your workouts at a specified pulse rate below your maximum. For distance workouts, try 40–60 beats below max, for intervals try 20–40 below max. For speed workouts you don't measure your pulse. For tempo workouts you should try and determine your optimal pulse rate. This is what pacing is all about. But more about that later.

The Problems

There are two main problems with any formula for pulse-rate averages for exercise. First, it's quite difficult to measure your pulse accurately, particularly your maximum. The instant you stop to count your heartbeat—you know, you feel on your wrist or your neck or over your heart to get the thumps, and then you wait for the second hand on your watch to come to a convenient point—your heart starts to slow down. By the time you finish your count your heart rate might be down as much as 5 to 15 beats a minute from its maximum. Second, supposing that you could get accurate readings of your heart rate at any time (you might have a monitor attached to yourself, or some such), then you are faced with the problem of trying to determine what your average rate is during your workout. On uphills you would expect a rate higher than average, on downhills a rate lower than average, and on the flats ——? From a strict mathematical approach you would have to determine how much time you spent at each heart rate in order to figure your average. Of course it's not intended that you try: these are just guides for heart rates.

Common Sense

I'm going to suggest another guide.

It's you.

Don't get too hung up on pulse rates in determining intensity of exercise. However, you can take out a watch occasionally and time yourself. See what you are working at on a tough uphill. See how soon your rate recovers considerably. Sometime when you seem to be going along very comfortably, in a steady state, check your pulse. Log all these figures; then in a few weeks do it again.

If you get a fair amount of information on your own heart rate during different bouts of exercise you can use these casual data as a check on yourself. You might be out plugging along, thinking you were working hard. If you took your pulse you might find it was a fair amount under what you had been able to tolerate previously, and hence if you want to get a better workout you should step up the pace in this instance.

General theories on intensity

A very good rule to follow during training is—

CPT 3: During a training period or season, increase the duration of your training first, and then as the training period nears an end, increase the intensity of training.

For instance, many skiers train steadily by running, beginning late in the spring and continuing until snow comes. During this time, under this schedule, it would be a good approach to build up the amount of distance done during spring and summer, even perhaps into early fall (this last would depend in part on when you were expecting to get on snow). Thereafter and until snowtime, the distance should be held constant and the intensity increased. Thus if your distance workouts got to around 15 km by, say mid-September, you would not increase them, but run them faster.

Or, if you worked up to a certain number of intervals you would then keep the number steady and increase the intensity, by running them faster or cutting down the rest periods in between, etc.

An athlete who trains this way, with a steadily increasing intensity, will probably be able to perform fairly consistently during the racing season.

There is another approach to this idea of increasing extent and then intensity, and for that I invite you to read the discussion on peak periods in Chapters 10 and 14.

CPT 4: One of the characteristics of all living things, including the human body, is its ability to respond to a stimulus.

You train hard and in doing so send a signal to your body, which in turn reacts and adjusts to the load. You work harder and harder and your body responds more and more.

Well, that's what it's all about, this training.

CPT 5: It is easier to stay in shape than to increase your fitness.

Some physiologists have determined that a decent workout twice a week will do a good job of maintaining the status quo. I believe this, and it's an important precept to remember during those periods when, for one reason or another, you can't train more often. But remember that you will have to train harder in order to up your conditioning. Don't get lulled into a state of complacency if you want to improve.

Value of anaerobic training

Recalling the definition of anaerobic work as that which produces so-called oxygen debt, or causes you to go under if continued long enough, the question arises: How much of this kind of training is good or necessary?

There is no clear answer to this. I tried hill climbs with poles for the U.S. Team for many years, thinking these anaerobic workouts were good. There is no doubt that 40–90-second hill climbs, done hard, are the toughest exercises going and can bring anyone to his knees. One theory holds that by training the anaerobic processes you can increase your ability to go faster under such extremely demanding conditions. Or you can build your tolerance for lactate in the system—lactate equaling pain in this case.

I don't know. There is probably some value in doing these tough hill climbs. Specifically, there is a mental toughening that is good for some people. But I now believe that if too many tough hill climbs are done there are the following risks. First, it's easy to build a dislike for this workout; and if you begin dreading the workouts that isn't good. Second, you may begin to ease off in your hill climbs in order to avoid pain; and then you are fooling yourself. Third, this sort of workout is termed a destructive one, where some of the cells of the body are actually destroyed; and there is real doubt as to the value of such destruction. Finally, and though it is a bit way-out, I believe that if hill climbs are done in excess the athlete will build in an automatic, psychological reaction which will force him to slow down to a point where the speeds can be tolerated more easily. This reaction is not to be confused with a conscious effort to slow down: I think the reaction is unconscious, but automatic.

There are still plenty of situations where extreme efforts are called for. In a race, if you know the course and know you have the ability to recover adequately, you really should attack the last parts of the uphills, and then recover on the downhill sections. Of course if you go under and do not recover you will lose time. So you train by sprinting up and over the tops of the hills, and then checking your recovery.

But after those tough hill climbs we used to do we were so tired that all we could do was stumble back down the hill, or rest. This is too intense, or going under too far, and I think it should be avoided in racing and in training, both. Since nearly 100 percent of a long-distance race is run under steady-state conditions, it makes sense to train in steady state (or aerobically, as many refer to it).

The best place to use an anaerobic effort is at the end of the race. You sprint for the finish and then take the consequences.

Finally, I highly recommend 10–12-second hill sprints (described in Chapter 9). These are primarily speed- and strength-builders, but they may have as much value in improving the anaerobic processes as the longer periods of anaerobic work—if there is any improvement to be gained at all.

Aerobic training

As I have said, most of your training must be done in a steady state, where you don't go under. One nice way of putting this is to say that a reduction of speed means less fatigue, which in turn means you can increase your volume of work each training session. There's no doubt that the volume of training is important.

The trends are toward increasing volumes. It's almost unbelievable. For example, during November 1978 many athletes logged 1500–2000 km skiing. At this writing, the top skiers in the world are averaging nearly 1000 km of training—mainly roller-skiing, hiking, running, and snow skiing—per month for twelve months of the year.

There is a fine line we must recognize between volume and intensity. You might say that you were going to walk 20 miles a day, which would be quite a volume. But it wouldn't do much for you, and it would take a long time too. A fellow would be better off running less far, but running with some intensity. I'll suggest some schedules in Chapter 14 and will say more about intensity in the section on peaking in Chaper 10.

Best ways to train

Most sports or exercises which utilize large muscle-groups are more pleasurable than activities which use fewer muscles. Wouldn't you rather get a workout by rowing, running, skiing, etc., than by pulling on armbands? You just can't get that feeling of over-all body relaxation after an armband workout.

Further, physiologists have actually determined that the best exercises are exactly those pleasurable ones which do use the largest muscle-groups. Lucky thing for all of those people who run, row and ski. In rowing a shell, for instance, it's quite easy to reach your max O_2 uptake. In fact, the de-

10. Jim Galanes, Chris Osgood and Tim Caldwell starting their weekly roller-ski up Mt. Ascutney, Vermont, during the fall of 1978.

mands of rowing are probably higher than those of running, but both exercises use the large muscle-groups, and hence mean more requirements for O_2.

And this in turn means better training.

Motivation

CPT 6: Ya gotta wanna do it.

Most of the exercise programs set up in this country are determined by coaches or school situations. From a young age on we are told, "It's time for Phys. Ed class . . . Now we are going to train . . . When I blow the whistle you begin . . ." And so on. Students, especially, are given little latitude in the types of training they can do, or in choosing the periods of time to do them in.

Since most of the instruction comes from paid coaches (who usually double as teachers in a school situation), most athletes think "this is the way it is, this is the way it should be"; and they even seek similar situations after leaving school. If some student athletes do try to strike out on their own they are often thwarted in one way or another by so-called top-level coaches. (Ways to instill motivation through variety are noted throughout the following chapters, and especially in 6 and 14.)

There is a very fine line to be drawn between coaches and athletes in the setting-up and performing of a training program. Coaches should offer suggestions or point out areas of weakness that need work. Coaches should be able to help organize and inspire the athletes, and to pick out technical flaws. But if you as an athlete go too far in accepting a coach's recommendations, or in depending on him to coax you out to train, or to bark orders and blow whistles for you, pretty soon you won't be doing it for yourself. Worse: If you rely on a coach who leaves the area, or if your opinion of him changes, your own program will suffer.

The feel of it

The human body is a very wonderful, complex mechanism and every day exercise physiologists are making strides in learning more about the body and how it performs under stress of work. Yet there will always be some unanswered questions. We may know more about the psychology than we do of the physiology. Who can say?

What allows an athlete to go out and have a fine performance one day, and then, several days later, apparently under the same circumstances, to go out and falter badly?

You may, better than anyone else, be able to figure out some of the answers to these questions. At any rate, you must try to, and one method which will help is to keep a training log like the one described in the next chapter.

Some of the top skiers of the world train themselves by feel. For instance, if their regular workout calls for some distance running and they don't feel up to it, they do something else. They are not bullheaded to the point that they follow through with their plan regardless. Nor are they ordered out by an inflexible coach.

However, the danger here is obvious. If athletes go soft on themselves and operate by a debased feel, they will lose out. Clearly, then, the top athletes don't go soft on themselves. They can tell the difference between feeling bad during a workout because they need the work, and feeling bad because they are run down or sick. If our top U.S. x-c skiers were to be judged as a whole I think we would find that they too often go out and bull it. This is because they do not know themselves well enough.

So I think there is quite a bit of room for that business called the individual approach to training. If there is one message I want to get across, it is this: Your own training program must be suited for you. Obviously it must be demanding, feasible, and all that, but the emphasis should be on the *you*. YOU gotta wanna do it.

11. Motivation. Period.

4. Progression & How to Log It

You'll hear that training programs should be progressive, and I want to explain what is meant by that.

Generally, if your program is progressive it means that your over-all workload or intensity increases during the months that you are training. Here are several statements which might sound contradictory, but actually should help to clarify things.

1. I recommend 2- to 4-week periods during the year when your program will *not* seem to be progressive. More about peaking in Chapter 10, but for now suffice it to say that during these periods your over-all load will not increase.

2. A progressive program does not mean one that shows an increased load *day by day*: this would be disastrous.

3. During certain seasons, such as the spring, your program might be hard to measure, or it might actually slack off in terms of workload. But with a progressive program you would expect to do more during one spring season than you did during the previous spring.

4. If you are advanced in age there is some point where you should stop worrying about progressing in pure workload terms. Think of it in another way: "If I can still do things at age 50 that I'm doing now I'll feel I have progressed." As I've said before, training is an individual matter, and the older you get, the more you should rely on yourself, not charts or graphs.

The Increments

One of the biggest disappointments for people beginning a training program is the apparent lack of progress. Often they try to up their workload too soon. For example, one person might start out jogging 5 km three or four times a week, then after two weeks try to cut down the time for that distance by as much as a minute or two. This in turn might be quite a strain on his body; he might go under or come home with sore muscles, and all that. Such results are discouraging and are not what I consider part of a progressive program.

So take the increments slowly. You shouldn't even think of a crash program. If you want to race, or train to get in shape, it won't be very meaningful to you unless you train for at least a year. After that time you can look back and see what you have accomplished and then judge your progress. Most physiologists count on 5 to 8 years of training as being necessary for an athlete to be really competitive in world-class endurance events like x-c ski racing.

In the meantime, set up your schedule so that the increments—the jumps, progressions, or whatever you want to call them—come once a month. A month is a good unit of time and easy to associate with. "I'll be running 5 k's this month and next month it will be 7 at the same speed." And so on.

In the beginning if your program seems too easy, don't worry. There are advantages to establishing yourself at an exercise level. Your muscles adapt to that load, your body can take it, you are less likely to get tired, run down or discouraged. I don't think there is much chance for deconditioning if you take an increment at the beginning of the month, reach it easily within two weeks, and then hold it for the last two weeks of the month.

If you can gain confidence in your ability to do the workload it will mean a lot for your whole program. It's called stabilization.

Number of Workouts

It's better to go out three times a week for six weeks than six times a week for three weeks. It goes back to the stabilization process I just mentioned. Don't rush things.

It's also better, if you have the time, to split the workload, after a point where you are doing a fair amount, to two workouts a day. Many top athletes take two workouts a day for an average of five or six days a week, right through the year. Normally the workouts are of different types: the athlete might do strength work in the morning and running in the afternoon, rather than doing everything in one wrap-up session.

Day On, Day Off

Probably the simplest, most easily understood method for determining the intensity of your workload on a given day is to follow the formula of one hard (or harder) day, then one easy (less hard) day. After a tough workout one day it's pretty hard to bounce back the next day for another grinder, so take it easy.

As they say, "Train, don't strain."

WEIGHT – 123 lbs. too much
PULSE – 40/38/36/37/39/39/38

Date	Flexibility	Strength	Skiing	Running	Rowing	Biking	Hillwork	Run/hike w/poles	Hiking	Other	COMMENTS
7/3	✓	45		70 min 8K		3/4 80k					Did circuits in the A.M. before hiking. Hats part way home. Nice day—helped make me feel good. P.M. jogged to loosen up and relax.
7/4			1:20 20k		1:10						A.M. Rollerskiing; didn't feel too snappy. P.M. Good row, but bad blisters!
7/5	✓	40						2:30 25K		tennis 1 hr	A.M. Circuits, finally improving. P.M. Busting it for 2½ hours – GREAT!! Incorporated hill-walking – or skiwalking.
7/6				30 6k	1						A.M. Waddled w/dog + fine row — HOT. P.M. Lazy–feels too hot to do much.
7/7	✓	45	1:25 20K	45							A.M. Circuits - fine. Don't ever roller ski in the heat of the day when P.M. it's like this!! Heat made it painful! Phew!!
7/8			45 6k				40 6k		45 5k		A.M. A scummy trip—rollerskied up—ok—at least no stops, walked down, ran/walked up, got a ride down, ruled up the hiking trail. Two trips is enough!! But I felt okay.
7/9	✓				50	2 57k					A.M. Good row with some pacing – fun. P.M. 2nd bike ride of the week – wow! Felt pretty good!
TOT		2:10	3½	1:10	3	5¼	40	2:30	45	19/hours	
ALS			46k	14k		137 K	6k	25 K	5k	233 ks (with biking)	tired at end of week, time for a rest day

12. This page from the training log of an aspirant to the U.S. Women's Team shows variety in her workouts—plus frank comments that will help to stabilize her workload.

If there is any question now regarding harder days *vs.* easier days, you'll soon learn to distinguish them as you train more.

Training Log

One of the most important parts of anyone's program is the keeping of a log or journal. I'll address the advantages to the athlete who wants to peak for certain races during the winter.

The log should contain, as a minimum, the following information: each day's workout and some comment on how it felt, hours of sleep, weight taken about once a week, and rested pulse rate. In addition, most athletes keep a running score of their various workouts in terms of time and distance. The kilometers run each day can be added weekly, then each week's sums can be totaled at the month's end, etc. (See the Equivalency Table in Chapter 14 for converting distances run, biked, rowed, etc., to a standard figure.)

The Day's Workout and How You Felt

There are very good reasons for keeping a log. First, you can look back in your log after a few months and see progress for yourself. Next, if you make some comments on your own condition it will give you some guide to the consequences of your workouts. For instance, "Those hill runs were real tough, especially after the fifth one." If you had a distance workout the day before and found your hill runs the next day too tough, your entries tell you something you may be able to apply to a racing situation.

That Winner's Day

If you train long enough you're going to begin to have what I call winner's days every so often. These are the days when you run right away from the people you're training with, or when you just can't seem to tire yourself by going at top speeds. I'll have more about this peaking in Chapter 10, on inseason training.

Put a star in your log for these days. The whole idea is to try to program these super occasions so they fall during race days. Sounds simple, but it may take years to learn this. You'll have to study all the days that led to your great effort, then try to duplicate it again and again. You might not get the formula right off, but keep working at it. Competition is so tough at the top levels that no one wins unless he has a winner's day.

Rested Pulse

Knowing your rested pulse can be a very valuable bit of information—if it is used correctly.

First, you must always take your pulse under exactly the same conditions. The best time to do so is immediately after you wake up. If you lie in bed, roll around, and begin thinking about the day's events, it's likely that your pulse will elevate and a reading of it might alarm you. Some athletes know their heart rates go up automatically when thinking about a race and therefore they don't even bother to take it on race days.

After you train for a few months your rested pulse rate should go down . . . unless it's already at its low.

The lowest pulse rate I'm acquainted with is Mike Elliott's. He went to a doctor one day for a check-up and his heart was bleeping along in the low 30's. The doctor thought Mike was a candidate for sick bay rather than for the Olympic Team. A fair number of athletes on the U.S. x-c team register rates in the 30's when they first wake up. But don't fret if

13.   And be sure to include all family tours in your training log.

yours isn't that low. I never got mine even into the 40's—it seems to plug along at 60 no matter how rested a state I'm in.

If you wake up with a slow pulse it generally means you are rested and ready to go. You can again check back in your journal and see what events preceded this low-pulse day. Then try to plug that information into your race schedule during the winter. You can experiment on this during the offseason too.

If you wake up and your pulse is higher than usual it could mean any of three things. First, you're excited about something or just woke up from a wild dream; second, the previous day's workout was a "bear" and you're tired; or third, it may be the onset of some sickness.

Whatever the cause, though, don't get psyched out by a slightly high pulse. If all athletes allowed their pulse rates to program their workouts and dictate race participation we would see a lot of inactivity and lots of did-not-starts.

Body Weight

Keeping an account of your weight should lead you to figure out your best skiing weight. It's also the simplest way to know if you are getting enough calorie intake. There's a simple principle: If your calorie intake exceeds your calorie output (the amount of calories you burn up by existing and exercising) you will gain weight. If the process is reversed you will lose weight.

Some of my doctor friends tell me that during a good training program your appetite decreases relative to your caloric demands, and this is the best, healthiest way to get your weight down to "a fighting trim." I'll buy that.

I'll say more about food in Chapter 11.

Hours of Sleep

You should find this useful in your over-all approach. If it seems necessary to get so many hours' sleep for two or three days preceding a good workout, plug this fact into your program.

Also, learning your sleep pattern over an extended period, particularly during travel, will help you to diagnose the reasons why it may vary on occasion, and you'll be less likely to get uptight about sleep before a race.

Memories, Too

If you keep an accurate and, I hope, helpfully descriptive log, it will provide you with a lot of pleasure as you look it over in the months to come. There just has to be a psychological boost in looking back and reading about those workouts which stood out in your mind.

I wonder that I ever did some of those things—like hiking 30 miles a day for nine days. But there it is, in print, and it makes fine reading.

And More

If you're the mathematical type, or like to draw graphs and charts, you can plot your pulse rate against your weight, your distance totals, and so on. This can prove very interesting.

Theoretically, your pulse should go down as you train, your workload should go up, and, if you're overweight, your weight should go down. If your weight doesn't go down it might be because you've lost fat and gained muscle, which is heavier, so don't worry about *that*.

In sum: A training log should be kept to provide you with useful information. The important matters are your progress, your distance figures, your over-all conditioning, and your ability to program or predict the circumstances which lead you to your best efforts. Body weight and rested pulse rates are not as important. I've seen lots of winners of the rested-pulse sweepstakes who don't come out on top of the finish list, so don't get obsessed with your facts and figures, or *especially anyone else's*. Use all this information as objectively as you can.

5. Interval Training

Some people claim that *interval* in the term *interval training* refers to the rests, or less physically demanding parts of the session, between the bouts of fairly tough effort. Others tell us that interval training encompasses the whole workout.

Not to worry. What matters is the underlying belief in the potency of interval training: that the body's system can be worked at a near-maximum level for a longer accumulated period of time than would casually seem possible. This is the theory most generally accepted for this sort of training. And therefore, since the best way for an athlete to improve his physical condition is to work at or near maximum effort, the argument goes, interval training is good.

Intervals can be done on foot, on skis, while biking, roller-skiing, rowing, or during many other kindred activities that require a large O_2 uptake.

Sample workout

A typical interval workout might go like this. A 4- or 5-minute loop is run at about 80-100 percent effort, putting the body under a stress that could not be maintained for so long as, say, 10 minutes. Then the loop is jogged once, rather easily, to give the body time to recover; then it is run again at the higher intensity. And so on.

The standard method for determining the number of loops to be run is by taking times. When the running or recovery loop times fall off quite a bit it's probably time to quit. Or, when your muscles feel stiff, tired, numb or sluggish. (If you run intervals on the same loop you won't need a watch after a while: you'll know when your times are slacking off and it's time to stop.)

There are hundreds of different interval workouts and this is just one example, but it will serve to continue the argument, which goes like this. A cross-country ski race can be considered a series of intervals. On the uphills the skier is working near maximum effort, continually flirting with the danger of going under. On the downhills he has a chance for partial or complete recovery. The flats are run at efforts in between these two. So why not train by running intervals?

As applied to x-c

Well, I have to agree. But I think that distance training is the most important kind of training for skiing. Distance training by my definition necessarily contains a series of intervals. (Try running around the countryside of the Green Mountain State, Vermont, without getting into some stress situation on hills, which are followed by recovery periods going downhill.) I'll say more about this in the section on distance training, but for now I would like to summarize some of the important differences between x-c skiing and track-running. So many interval-training programs are laid out for track-runners that it is worth noting these differences:

1. X-C skiing has more ups and downs, of irregular distances.

2. X-C skiing has more-nearly-complete recovery periods on the downhills.

3. X-C skiing requires more strength, especially in the upper body.

4. X-C skiing is usually done over longer distances. Except for the marathon, 10,000 meters is the longest official Olympic running distance, while 10,000 meters, or 10 km, is the shortest men's x-c racing distance.

One problem some of our skiers have had is that their training schedules were patterned after those for track-runners. As you can see, I think these are best left to the track people, especially in the matter of interval workouts.

Distance in interval

However, I have a hunch that lots of the people who have been arguing so long for one method of training or the other—interval or distance—have actually been doing both kinds of training, but simply haven't defined it that way. If a runner goes out interval training and runs 10 hard loops, taking 4 to 5 minutes each, and takes a recovery loop between each hard one, it might be understating it to say he had a distance workout. And if a skier went out for a distance workout and bounded around the countryside for about two hours, at a pace slightly faster than the recovery-loop pace of the first runner, he would probably get into quite a few stress situations on uphills which would be followed by recoveries, just like interval training.

Call it what you want, but let's agree to get into some stress situations during training. In running, biking or roller-skiing these will best be done on uphills.

How many, how far, how hard, where

For x-c ski training you must run intervals of at least 3 minutes, preferably more. It's fine to run loops and use the same one for a recovery loop. If jogging this loop seems too easy, run it a bit faster, or run a recovery loop that is shorter. Running a recovery loop is much preferred to standing around waiting to recover.

You should run the loop fairly hard, but not so hard that you go under, or that you cannot recover by jogging the loop afterward. Many athletes use pulse rate as an indicator of recovery. When the pulse is back down to 120 it's time to run another hard loop.

I don't recommend timing every running and recovery loop, but if you do so occasionally you will see some advantages. First, you can tell when your times fall off—in the event you can't feel it. Second, you will have some record for your log and something you can refer to for comparison in the months to come.

I run a little loop in the woods and about every two weeks I time myself just to see how it's going. During the spring and summer I simply try to increase the number of loops I run, and they take about 5:30 each. During the fall I hold the number of loops steady and try to run them faster. This is in line with the theory I expressed previously.

When you run intervals you should do them on varied terrain. This is most important. Stay away from flat-running situations if you can.

Where Does It Hurt?

Some coaches and athletes talk about the pain barrier, and training or conditioning oneself to be able to push back that barrier—i.e., to be able to take more and more pain. "No pain, no gain," they say.

I think that word *pain* should not be used in talking about training and racing. I've never heard the world's top racers talk about it, and the reasons they don't are easy to understand. For one thing, pain should not be considered an automatic ingredient of training: if it were, it might be too destructive, both in terms of physical conditioning and mental outlook. Next, in a race, pain is something to avoid. It usually means you have been running too hard and may be about ready to go under. And if you go under your time is bound to suffer.

Next try to get a loop in the woods or on other soft ground. It is more like the terrain you find in racing situations and it is also more rewarding, psychologically. Compare running in the woods with training on a hardtop or gravel road. The footing on the hard surfaces is firmer and requires little concentration, whereas in the woods it's likely to be a little uneven. But I say this unevenness is good, because it is more similar to a skiing situation where you have to concentrate with every stride. Running on slightly uneven ground will also develop the muscles that help you to maintain better balance. Soft ground is easier on the joints too.

Build a loop

Every training setup should have available a little training loop. I have seen these all over Europe and they are quite easy to build. The standard approach is to lay out a track of about 1 km through terrain in the woods. Then clear it, smooth it by digging out roots and rocks if necessary, and mark it. On some of the fancier loops a trench is dug to a depth of about 6–10 cm all the way around, which is filled with a combination of gravel and sawdust, or a similar mixture. This makes for very nice footing. Markers are placed every 50 meters along the trail and then if runners want to go hard for a couple of hundred meters some added incentive is right there.

I've watched athletes training on these loops in Europe and they really seem to enjoy it. Often two runners will alternate setting the pace, or one will run the fast loop and the other the recovery loop.

Naturally these loops also can be used for distance workouts, but a longer track would be preferable.

Various intervals

A *natural interval* is one which utilizes the terrain. For instance, you might take a run through terrain and go hard on the uphills, even walk the downhills, and run easily along the flats. This sort of workout puts the same stress on your system as skiing does and it is therefore highly recommended.

Many skiers run natural intervals in snow, skiing the uphills very fast, coasting the downhills, and cruising the flats. This is similar to a distance workout, even though, strictly speaking, a distance workout over the same terrain might call for less effort on the uphills.

Strength-speed intervals are designed to improve your strength and

14. Tempo training (plus technique, described in Chapter 16) produces the good one-step double-poling shown by these racers at the start of the men's World Junior Championship relay at Mont Ste-Anne, Québec, in February 1979.

speed, and I will cover them separately in chapters 8 and 9.

The *tempo workout* is an interval at racing speed and is usually done on snow during the winter. Because it is the purpose of the tempo workout to adjust the body to racing speed, the skier usually skis on gradual uphills for 5 to 10 minutes, then takes a complete recovery before doing it again. As a rule-of-thumb, tempo workouts should not exceed 1/5 the distance you are training for.

6. Distance Training

Because most training that is being done is distance training these days, people often don't use different terms to indicate variations on the main theme. They don't have to, I suppose, if their training is always distance training.

But I want to keep the different workouts clear in your mind, so I will be specific hereafter. I'll even throw in the term *distance/interval training* occasionally—meaning a distance workout that contains intervals, with the intervals often natural ones that are caused by the terrain.

Distance training is the meat and potatoes of any good training program in x-c skiing. Strict interval training, weight or strength training, co-ordination exercises, etc., are all good activities, but they aren't shortcuts or alternatives to this most necessary part of a correct program. The evidence of the value of distance training is simply overwhelming. It develops the ability to maintain a steady state of exercise at continually higher rates of intensity, it develops endurance, and it develops the ability to withstand fatigue. No successful x-c skier is without these attributes.

I have already covered interval training and have remarked that proper distance training includes intervals or series of differing periods of intensity. This is very important to realize, so you'll know what I mean if I refer to distance/interval training hereafter.

There are all sorts of distance workouts and I will handle them separately. My list is not exhaustive. But first there are a few general points to cover.

Pacing, intensity

Pacing is inherent in the idea of distance training. Many athletes have difficulty pacing themselves during workouts or races. I am a prime example. I usually start out too fast, or hit the first hill too hard, and go under. Then I suffer for a long time afterward, trying to recover. I might add that I go pretty slowly during that time of recovery, too!

So don't go out and blow it right at the beginning. If you're taking a running workout it's quite easy to warm up by jogging slowly. After you heat up a bit do a few stretching exercises, jog some more, then increase your pace—slowly—slowly. If you feel yourself starting to go under (my legs get numb, my chest feels constricted or my breathing increases and gets very loud), slow down.

Don't hesitate to walk up a steep hill. The best skiers in the world walk

15. An old logging road, clipped and raked, makes an ideal training track for any season.

or ski-stride up hills during their distance workouts, especially in the summer. So don't feel like the Lone Ranger if you walk occasionally.

The Key to Pacing

Remember the most important part of pacing. It's better to finish your workout feeling you could do more, or that you could have gone a bit harder, rather than to finish struggling, tired, or hanging on. You've got to put yourself in a frame of mind that will make you "wanna do it" again.

How long

The length of a distance workout depends on the intensity and the type of exercise, of course. It is also very dependent on your own conditioning.

In general, for a running workout you should consider a time twice as long as a short event you're training for, and a time up to as much as you'd need for a race of 30 to 50 k's. Sounds broad, but let me explain.

If you are training for a 20-minute race, a workout of 40 minutes' running wouldn't be excessive. However, if you are training for a 50-km race, where the time runs close to three hours, a training run of six hours would be a bit much, to say the least. Something less intensive than running—hiking or biking—would be better for these longer workouts. You can also estimate the time you should be spending on distance by using simple arithmetic. Refer back to your training log (Chapter 4), then look at the suggested schedules in Chapter 14.

Where

The best place to take a distance workout is over terrain similar to x-c trails, or on x-c trails themselves, if that is possible. (I'm going to talk about biking and rowing and naturally you wouldn't get very far on most x-c trails on a bike or in a shell.)

Most x-c trails in this country are not suited for running. This is because the footing is hazardous or because skiers think road-running is better and therefore don't prepare the trails for foot-running. In time this attitude will change. Running over a trail offers the advantages I have mentioned before—it's similar to skiing terrain, it's easier on the joints, and it's psychologically more rewarding. The advantage of building foot and ankle strength by running over terrain can be somewhat offset if the terrain is rough and you are likely to twist an ankle. I'm not recommending you run through rough stuff: just that you fix yourself a nice running track in the woods, or over good terrain.

Long loops are preferable to shorter ones because you get less bored. The feeling of accomplishment after a long trip is important too. Come in and think about where you have run (or look at a map, if you have to) and it will give you a sense of well-being.

Still, many skiers pound the roads for training. This is tolerable at a young age but it isn't too imaginative. And when you get older you'll be looking for that softer ground. I can guarantee that.

Lighter people can withstand the jarring produced by road-running better than heavier people. If you want a good example of this, study some of the marathoners. Not many of them weigh over 140 pounds and few, if any, are in the 180-pound bracket. In x-c skiing, though, there is an interesting trend toward bigger skiers. Many of the top racers in the world now look like split ends for a professional football team, being well built, tall and rangy. And I don't see many of them running long distances on hard surfaces—they can't take it because of their body weight.

The Three R's

CPT 7: The three best distance workouts are running, rowing, and roller-skiing.

Each of these involves the use of a large mass of muscles in the body, each can be psychologically rewarding, and each has certain direct connections with skiing. If you stuck to the Three R's during the year you would have plenty of variety and I'm sure you would get in good shape. I'm not eliminating such activities as biking and hiking either, but I think you get more for your money's worth with the Three R's.

Running

The distance-running workout is the most popular form of training and there's little doubt that it will continue to be so. It takes less equipment than any other form of good distance training, anyone can do it just about anywhere, and it's intensive enough so that it doesn't require long periods of time to complete. Intervals, natural or other kinds; speed play (unscheduled bursts of speed; what the Swedes call *fartlek*)—ski-striding and ski-bounding all can be incorporated into a running workout. These latter exercises are discussed more fully in Chapter 7 and in Chapter 17 on uphill technique. If you're worried about the arms and upper body you can station a few Putney armbands—those blown-out, bicycle-tire innertubes—along your route and stop to yank on them.

It's easy to go out alone, and then it's all you. No equipment to get in shape, no weather to worry

16. Dianne Holum—U.S. skating coach, and 1972 Olympic gold medalist—Joe McNulty, formerly of the U.S. x–c Team, in a distance workout.

about, no skis to wax. You can leave your worries behind and go. Running, done properly, is a free expression and nearly addictive.

The only disadvantages are that long distances or running on hard surfaces can cause stiffness, sore muscles, or slight damage to the joints; running is not the best activity if you're recovering from some lower-body injury.

For long runs try a variety of running forms. Don't just go out and pound out the kilometers, come in and say "There, that's over." You have to train with a difference.

Uphills

Because uphill skiing comprises about half the time spent during a race you should concentrate on hills. Do your "think-training" here.

After a warm-up establish your pace. Then do some ski-bounding on the first uphills. If this bounding gets tiring, do some ski-striding—which is a bit like an elongated walking step. Old-fashioned straight uphill running, especially off a flat foot or off your heel, will not do so much for you as ski-bounding and ski-striding. I think that you will find ski-bounding strenuous enough so you won't feel you are cheating yourself in terms of a good workout. Another interesting method for going up the hills is to try to use the muscles in your upper leg and abdomen as much as possible. This is best done walking

or bounding along at a fairly slow pace, and involves a slight straightening at the waist with each step. The largest, strongest muscles in your body are located here and if you can use them to climb hills, all the better. There is a skiing technique for climbing hills which utilizes these muscles too.

It's a good idea to hyperventilate before starting up the hills. Many skiers do this until they get dizzy and they claim it helps with their oxygen supply. Then try to pace yourself on the hill so you come off the top with more speed than you started with. For a long uphill you might use several different running techniques. You could start ski-bounding; and if this affects you as it does me your knees will get tired. You could then shorten your stride a bit and use the calf muscles more, until they get tired. Then perhaps some vigorous ski-striding would be in order; then maybe that walk or jogging bound using the abdomen muscles as much as possible. Then you could start all over with ski-bounding, perhaps. You will be able to adjust and use different movements according to the steepness and length of the hill—but try to tax every muscle in your lower body. It's just like shifting gears in a truck in order to get up the hill.

Conjecture: A shift in techniques on long uphill stretches will relax you and make you more efficient in terms of O_2 consumption.

58

Downhills

There isn't much point in rushing down a hill during training. If you're on hard pavement it can be especially jarring. If you're on slightly rough terrain you run the risk of a fall. An easy jog or even a walk down steep hills is fine. The training effect gained from running down hills is not significant.

If you slow up for a long time going down a big hill you may need to start in again at the bottom rather slowly. You might also be fooling yourself if you counted this time as part of a cardiovascular workout.

The Flats

When you are running along in a steady state, through the woods, you should have a flowing feeling. It's wonderful to be at one with the surroundings when even every breath seems to fit in with part of the landscape. Really. Sometimes I imagine myself as actually part of the trail, the leaves, roots and rocks on the ground, the trees and ridges

17. A good program of foot-running pays off during the next winter's competitions.

around the area, and I hate to tear myself away. I suppose runners can get the same feeling out in the open, or on a track, but I've been lucky enough to have woods to run in.

If you come onto some long flats you can do speed-play or *fartlek*, and run at high speeds for as long as you feel good.

Or you can pick out a point ahead and sprint for it, then gear down a bit and continue at your old established pace.

A very interesting, popular set of intervals that many runners use is a progressive system of harder runs. They might start and go hard for 200 meters, then ease off; go hard for 400 meters, ease off; and so on, up to 1400–1600 meters, then come back down the scale. You wind up steadily, then wind down, just like a giant engine that you don't want to treat wrong by stepping it up too fast, or slowing down too fast.

Precautions

There is plenty of material available on equipment for running and I don't want to spend much time on that here. Naturally your shoes should be broken in before you take any long runs. Some runners have special arrangements for socks— some need tape to prevent blisters. Some use special powders or ointments to prevent chafing. These are all tricks you can pick up if you get in with the running crowd.

Most important of all, take running for the good things it offers you. Don't get hung up if you run with a group and can't keep up. Some of the best runners in the world can't ski, and some of the best skiers in the world can't run well either. If ski races were decided on foot-running abilities there wouldn't be any sense in having ski meets, would there? So remember, running is an excellent cardiovascular workout. If you can combine it with ski-striding and ski-bounding, all the better.

Rowing

Rowing in a shell with a sliding seat is one of the Three R's because it demands the use of so many of the body's muscles. The pulling and pushing of the arms is probably more valid for x-c than most weight-lifting exercises. There is little question about the value in using the abdomen and back muscles in rowing. And the real sleeper is the use of the legs: When they straighten out during the stroke the motion is very similar to the straightening of the legs in skiing.

The Central Europeans have long

18. Rowing is getting more popular for x–c training: in the strip opposite, two women racers head upstream on the Connecticut River near Putney. Note their flexion, compared with the kayaker's confined lower body in Photo 19.

19. A kayaker's legs are rigidly braced.

sity. That's easy. You can go hard for a while, then ease up. You can control your own distance/interval training.

If you use rowing for a lot of your training it would be a good idea to add a good ration of toe rises for the ankle and lower leg muscles. These are not used in rowing as much as in skiing or running. They are small muscle groups, but very important. (See section on toe rises in Chapter 9.)

The biggest disadvantage to rowing is the equipment and accessibility. Not everyone lives close to water, and of those who do, not many have access to rowing shells. However, the sport is increasing in popularity partly due to the fiberglass construction, etc. (as in kayaking). I think that in time many more skiers will be taking up this sport.

It's fine to hitch a fishing line on the shell too. See if the fish can catch you!

*   *   *

The third R, roller-skiing, is covered separately in Chapter 7, the one on specificity.

used rowing in training, but some of our skiers interpreted "rowing" as kayaking, or paddling—where the legs are immobilized, and hence don't get the needed workout.

Some purists criticize rowing because the body, as in biking, is supported, while in running or skiing the antigravity muscles—the ones that hold us upright—are being used all the time. However, it's probable that more muscle mass is used in rowing than in any other sport, and this factor is very good for training purposes. It goes back to the old example: Are you going to get a good workout sitting in a chair and lifting something fairly heavy with one arm, or will you get a better workout using nearly all the muscles in the body rather vigorously? You know the answer. Chalk up one for rowing.

Since there are no uphills and downhills in rowing you have to make your own, in terms of inten-

For extra variety
Hiking

To go hiking in the mountains is a privilege not enjoyed by enough athletes. If you have access to good hiking terrain you should take several jaunts a year, for pleasure and for training. Hiking is one of the great exercises that has practically no disadvantages, and it will always be that way.

If you are alone you can set your own pace. I remember that doing the distances in ⅓ the prescribed guidebook times seemed to give a good workout. But that was quite a rush. Now I would prefer to take a pack with food or other weight in it and go at a more leisurely pace, yet still get a good workout.

20. Rugged terrain in Bessengen, Norway, adds to the workout on a morning hike.

If you are in a group you can be the one to take the pack. And if there are all sorts of eager beavers who want to carry the pack for extra training, take along one of your own and fill it with rocks. How many mountains have you been up where some people were making an effort to raise the altitude a few feet by carrying rocks to the top? I know mountains which fall a few feet short of an even thousand feet and it has always been one of the jokes to try and raise the level. Well, it's a gimmick, but all good programs have a few gimmicks.

The uphills provide the best test, as usual. Ski-striding and ski-bounding are in order for these sections. The downhills should be taken with caution. I would advise against carrying heavy loads downhill: the continual holding-back can cause too much strain on the legs.

Hiking is so much fun that you almost feel that it can't be good training. I remember one kid who used to hike a lot and then he took up x-c skiing. His coach told him that he had to train hard, get out there and suffer, and that hiking was good for ski training. Well, the fun went out of it for the kid when he started to be so concerned with the training aspect of hiking, rather than the pleasures of hiking; so he gradually quit it. Now he's stopped skiing too.

Hiking a few mountain ranges ranks with taking a long tour on skis. These are some of the supreme moments in exercising and the more of them you do, the happier you'll be. (Psst! You'll get in shape too.)

Orienteering

Orienteering combines running or hiking through terrain with map-and-compass reading. This sport has long been used by the Scandinavians for ski training and it's been catching on here on this side of the Atlantic, with orienteering clubs proliferating since the first North American Championships were held in Carbondale, Illinois in 1971.

You'd be well advised to try orienteering, if you haven't already. It is marvelous training and puts you in another frame of mind. When you're competing, or after you're finished, you just feel different. It's difficult to explain that feeling but it isn't anything like the other normal training you do. One reason for this might be the requirement for thinking during orienteering. Don't underestimate the need for using your brain or for concentrating. Many a skier, eager for a workout, has been lost while orienteering. And if you're lost in an orienteering race, well . . .

Ice Skating

Although not many skiers do much ice skating, this is another good exercise. In our area we often have good ice (especially the "black ice") before the snow flies and we always try to get out. The rhythm in skating is similar to skiing, it's wonderful for your balance, and it provides another good diversion in the training schedule.

Biking

The use of biking as training for x-c skiing is a wonderful illustration of CPT 1 and CPT 2. I don't think it offers the training potential that the Three R's do, and my belief is based on these reasons:

1. In biking, the body is supported and you do not use the large group of muscles required by any of the Three R's. (In rowing, recall, even though the body is supported, many of the upper-body muscles, as well as those in the legs, are used.)

2. A lot of biking is likely to develop large thigh muscles, which are of little use in x-c skiing. In fact, excessively large muscles can be a hindrance to the skier. Biking can also lead to a stiff back.

Other Disadvantages

There are other disadvantages to biking. Let me list these, before I turn around and tell you why so many skiers do bike as part of their training program.

Biking can be dangerous. Many of our top U.S. skiers have suffered injuries through spills.

Biking is not really a specificity exercise.

Weather is a prohibiting factor. During cold or wet weather, biking must be avoided.

Equipment is expensive and equipment problems themselves can be frustrating.

Nevertheless . . .

However, lots of skiers take to their bikes during the early spring and summer months for all the advantages that biking does offer.

Biking is a very good diversion. Some athletes get tired of running all year round. Biking can be more exciting and enjoyable. Large distances can be covered in a day. (During a bike tour the U.S. Team skiers were able to cover over 160 km a day with ease, for eight consecutive days.)

Since the body is supported in biking this means less strain on the ankles and knees. Therefore it's a

21. Food on the fly for U.S. Team members during an 800-mile training tour.

marvelous exercise for someone who may be recovering from certain leg injuries, or for someone who has brittle joints that suffer from a lot of running.

During long bike rides there are two features remarkably similar to x-c skiing. One is the need for feeding, or replacing liquids and food burned by the body. So biking is a good way to train yourself for feeding. The other feature which is often overlooked is the need for concentration during biking. If you're riding in a pack you must be alert at all times, being sure to stay in position, to be in the right gear, to watch the road for small bumps or ruts, and to be ready to take the lead and expend a high amount of energy. (See section on concentration in Chapter 15.)

Hilly terrain can offer the distance/interval training demands necessary for x-c. We have some courses around home which are ideal for that. There are several short uphills followed by flats and downs which require that straight-ahead, steady, hard effort.

Most skiers claim that standing up on bikes so as to pump uphill utilizes the same muscles and motions used in skiing uphills. You will notice that you can get quite a bit of power off the ball of your foot when standing up on the bike.

In sum: Biking is a good form of exercise. Since following a biker, or utilizing his windbreak, makes it 15 to 20 percent easier to pedal, biking is an event where the stronger bikers can go ahead and break wind for the weaker ones and everyone can hang together and still have a good workout. It is quite an equalizer.

22. Bill Koch (left) and Tim Caldwell pumping up a hill on part of a tri-state bike tour that will take them 100 k's in three hours. Their body positions are similar to those used in uphill skiing.

Top skiers in our corner of Vermont have acquired a reputation in the bike industry for destroying more cranks per 1000 km than any other cyclists in the world; this is because of the extreme pressure exerted on the cranks by bikers standing in this position. Your usual racing cyclist does more sitting on uphills and is smoother with his pumping motion.

7. Specificity Training

A few years ago specificity was a new trend in training, almost a fad. Now it's so accepted that many athletes and coaches don't even use *specificity* to describe this type of work. (Though maybe it's because the word is such a cat to pronounce.)

Anyway, most of the seasonal sports I'm acquainted with have some form of specificity training, particularly in the offseason. And you really don't have to use the word so long as you use the method.

The x-c skiers have always been in a peculiar situation. For training, if you're a foot-runner you can run all year, if you're a swimmer you can swim all year, but if you're a skier the only way you can ski all year is by going to a place like Australia during their winters, which are our summers. And this is a bit impractical for most x-c'ers I know.

So quite a long time ago the Putney skiers began their own specificity program, although then it didn't have the fancy name. First it was simply the use of armbands during the summer. Then ski-striding and ski-bounding came along and were incorporated into hikes or runs during the offseason. Now roller-skiing is here, and you can't get much more specific than that without actually being on snow.

There is no question of the value of specificity training. The more of it you can include in your schedule the better. And this brings up the following related point.

Which Exercises?

In training you should concentrate on the dominant feature of your event.

There may be disagreement between coaches and athletes as to the dominant feature of x-c racing. Is it endurance and conditioning, or is it technique and pacing? If it were simply endurance and conditioning one could train for x-c skiing much the same way an x-c foot-runner does, adding a few exercises for the upper body. If, on the other hand, x-c racing were primarily a technique and pacing event, an athlete would be well advised to train on these aspects during the year. Clearly, a good racer is strong in *all* aspects and he cannot slight any of them.

If there has been a fault with our program in the United States, I would say it has been with the lack of emphasis on technique and pacing. There has been too much emphasis on intensity at the expense of learning good techniques in training and skiing. By training on technique and pacing there is bound to be some spin-off value in conditioning (often quite a bit, in fact), but the converse is not always true.

It goes back, in part, to the corollary to CPT 2—you should put emphasis on training your weaknesses, especially during the offseason.

First Things First

The specificity exercises I list below are the best offseason training routines you can do. Most of the exercises qualify as strength builders, most of them will tax your O_2 uptake, and all of them will help your technique. They are really bonus exercises.

But remember, pay close attention to developing the proper form for the exercises first, then later building up the intensity with which you do them. This is training with a difference.

Ski-bounding

Ski-bounding is an uphill running exercise usually done at a tempo slightly slower than that of regular skiing. But an effort is made to simulate as much as possible the actual skiing movements. This means

23. Excellent form like this will carry over to winter racing.

24 & 25. The Brothers Koch—Bill (left in both cases) and Fritz—do some hill-striding, then take off for a 50-km round trip on roller skis in late October.

coming off the ball of the forward foot with a certain amount of aggressiveness and momentum, reaching forward with the arm as in diagonal (single stride) skiing, landing fairly flat-footed on the other leg and almost simultaneously rolling forward onto the ball of that foot and springing off it, etc.

One small error is to land on the ball of the foot instead of landing on a flat foot. In skiing uphill one of the keys is to set your wax and this is best done by having the ski flat, in contact with a maximum amount of snow. Then you press down on the ski . . . and hope. All this is done very quickly and automatically by top skiers. In fact, it's done so quickly that it may escape notice of the casual observer. If you land flat-footed while ski-bounding you will be more nearly imitating the skiing motion. On steep uphills it will not be possible to land with a flat foot, so don't worry about landing on the ball of your foot.

As you ski-bound pay particular attention to bending the forward ankle and collapsing or compressing slightly on the forward knee. This cushioning is an important part of uphill skiing. Some skiers straighten the rear leg behind to simulate the so-called kicking action of the diagonal technique. This is O.K., but I think it's more valuable to try to straighten your leg as much as possible while it's still underneath you.

Poles may be used, or not. I prefer them since it is more like skiing, and there is an added aerobic value to using them.

While you won't be getting up the hill quite so fast as a foot-runner in a hurry, I think if you do a little ski-bounding you will find it rather challenging as an exercise. We have a little hill here called Caldwell's Backyard Hillclimb and a few trips up this one, ski-bounding, seem to be enough for the toughest guys around.

Ski-striding

This is more similar to a walking motion but the effort here is made to simulate the body position and movements that are made during skiing the single stride. The tempo is slower than that of ski-bounding and many place the emphasis on a strong rear-leg kick.

Ski-striding is probably one of the most underestimated or least-used exercises in training. It's really one of the best. Consider running up a long hill, so long that you begin to tighten up or go under. Do you think you will gain by continuing to try and run? Definitely not. But if you break into a ski-stride you will be more able to keep going and keep your cardiovascular system working at a very high rate. The spin-off value gained is that you will be exercising your skiing muscles instead of *trying* to exercise

70

your foot-running muscles.

Naturally, ski-bounding and ski-striding can be done during almost any part of a hike or run. If you want to make ski-striding more effective just put a pack full of weights on your back.

The most important techniques in these two exercises are getting the thrust, or next move, from a rolling forward of the body, and specifically the appropriate leg, over the ball of the foot. This implies a certain amount of forward ankle-bend in the exercising leg. The most typical fault is bounding or striding off a flat foot. This won't do. Good skiing technique does not permit this motion, and therefore it's taboo in specialized training.

Armbands

Armbands—those elastic cords, or ropes which are pulled against some traction device—are a good training device because they can be set up almost anywhere, anytime, and using them will improve the strength and technique of your poling action.

The usual controversy exists about the use of armbands: Is it light resistance and many repetitions, or few reps and heavy resistance? It is most common to use

26. This strip shows excellent use of the racer's arms as she ski-strides uphill with a technique that will transfer to advantage on snow.

armbands with a higher degree of resistance during the summer "to build strength," and then as the snow season approaches to lighten the resistance and increase the number of reps "to increase endurance."

As you might guess, I don't completely favor this approach. I prefer using armbands with a fair amount of resistance—about as much as I can handle for 2 or 3 minutes—all year round. There are two reasons for this. First, I have never found endurance the main limiting factor in poling during an x-c race: rather, it has been strength. Second, in the interest of time I think it is more efficient to use armbands with a good deal of resistance. I've seen skiers work with armbands for 30 minutes and I'm not sure they get much out of it. They might have been better off doing an exercise that used a larger group of muscles, like roller-skiing, or hill-climbing with poles.

Kinds of Armbands

Factory-produced shock cords are available, some with good handles, others that you have to adjust or fix yourself by putting on a ski pole handle. Some skiers buy their own shock cord and make up a few sets of armbands.

The Norwegians have come out with an interesting rig that's nothing more than nylon line wrapped around a metal device. The more wraps, the more resistance.

The Exergenie is also a good rig, because it can be used at almost any setting of resistance. It's easily carried and set up—door jambs are good places—and therefore is a favorite for taking on extended trips.

Then there are the "Putney armbands"—homely, but cheap and expendable. Just get over to the nearest bike dealer and pick up a bunch of his blown-out bicycle innertubes and nail them up wherever

27. Tracey Thompson, 1975 Vermont high-school girls' 100- and 200-yard dash champion, skis x–c during her offseason. Here she works out on the Norwegian nylon line to strengthen her poling action.

you want them. We scatter them around trees in the woods and when we're out running we can stop and give a few pulls on them.

There are two basic differences between types like the shock cords or Putney armbands and the ones like the Exergenie and the Norwegian fixture. First, friend, there is no double-poling possible with the Exergenie type. (If you want to penalize skiers who are late to a workout, give them twenty double-poles on the Exergenie!) Second, the initial pull required for the shock-cord type is very slight, but then the resistance increases as your arm passes the body. *This is quite unlike real poling action,* where the main effort is expended at the beginning of the poling stroke.

Well, you can't have everything.

How to Do It

Most skiers have their armbands set up too low. It's a good idea to have them hitched up at head level, or higher, since this will develop the stronger poling motions, whether it's single-poling or double-poling.

Single-poling

Keep your elbows in as you use armbands. Don't cock your wrist to start the action. Make the initial effort with a strong pull *downward,* not backwards. Some skiers get into the bad habit of pulling backwards

because there is too much tension on the cords.

It's a good idea to have someone watch you once in a while. He can observe these things and also see if you have any extra quirks such as upper-body motion, a dropping of the shoulder, a twist of the hip, side-bending, etc. All these should be avoided: they're flaws (i.e., losses in efficiency) that can be carried over to your skiing technique.

Double-poling

During double-poling exercises you should get an upper-body motion. I tell skiers to pull with their arms to a point where their hands are about level with their hips and then to "statue" it the rest of the way: meaning to get the upper body into it—at least until the arms are past the body.

On-snow Applications

You can do all these exercises on snow and provide yourself with any amount of resistance. Simply stand on your skis on the level and single-pole without using any leg motion. Or double-pole. If this is too easy, get on an uphill section and repeat. You'll get the message.

The roller board

The roller board is a relatively new addition to our training devices and is considered by most coaches and athletes to be superior to armbands for training, especially in the double-poling motions.

The one shown below cost about $13.00 and two hours' carpentry to build. The 5/8-inch plywood section upon which the sled rides is braced underneath by 2 x 4's; its outside dimensions are 10 feet (about 3 m) long x 1 foot (30 cm) wide (if the sled is wider than 1 foot it will not accommodate the natural position of

28. In the frames below, Mary Heller-Osgood shows good form on the homemade roller board set up in the Caldwells' gym—also known as The Great Outdoors. The lower picture shows better the guides on the edges and the stop near the bottom of the slide.

the arms when they are used for real double-poling). Small guides are tacked on the outside edges of the plywood to steer the movable sled, and there is a stop for the sled 18 inches (45 cm) from the bottom.

The sled itself is also plywood, covered with leftover carpeting; it has four common furniture casters fixed to the bottom, each wheel being brazed to prevent it from swiveling when the sled is pulled up the slide, or let back down the slide from the uppermost position. The sled measures 1 foot x 32 inches (30 x 80 cm). The ropes the skier pulls on are attached at the upper end of the slide, with ski-pole straps as handles.

Clearly, the board can be slanted at any angle, depending on how hard you want to work. It is better to do 10 or more repetitions with correct form than to struggle with bad form while doing fewer reps at a steeper angle. When the initial pull is made, the hands and forearms should pull downward as well as back. It's a mistake simply to pull straight back with the arms, because this is not effective poling motion: You're missing that important downward thrust.

There may be some unwanted muscle development due to the force used in letting yourself slowly back down the slide. However, most skiers I know are content with this apparatus. Some use it by sitting,

instead of lying, on the sled. You should try both positions to see which suits you best.

Three sets of repetitions, doing about 75 percent of your maximum during the first two sets, and your maximum number during the last set, seem to work well. You will need rest between each set, and could do some other strength training for your legs, back, and abdomen in the meantime.

Roller-skiing

I don't know who invented roller skis but someone probably saw kids roller-skating or skate-boarding and figured that with one or two adjustments he could come up with a device for summer training that would approximate x-c skiing. The adjustments are easy to picture, and require x-c bindings and some ratcheted wheels that spin in only one direction.
poles and you're all set to go.

If an x-c skier had to choose only one type of training to do during the offseason he would probably be wise to roller-ski. In our corner of Vermont we have been roller-skiing for many years, and the more we do it the more important it seems. Interestingly, the Scandinavians have been slower to take this up than the Americans or some of the Central Europeans. The Scandinavians also believed for some time that the primary benefit of roller-skiing was for training the upper body and arms, so they spent most of their time on roller skis doing the double-pole. But now they appear to be doing more than that.

The Types

There are all sorts of roller skis, and to list the ones available at this time would only pose a problem to you, because in a year or so there will be newer models on the market, and some of the ones presently in vogue will no longer be around. Ski coaches are the best source of information for obtaining roller skis since these items are not carried regularly by many ski shops. Meanwhile, suffice it to say this:

You can get roller skis that are quite fast and easy to push along. You can get them with different sets of wheels which can be switched according to your needs. (Generally, these skis come with two sets of wheels and the smaller ones are used when you want more resistance in moving the skis.) You can get roller skis that are easy to maintain balance on, or ones that are difficult. Some skis can be used on smooth lawns or fairways, while most of the others are suitable for hardtopped pavements only.

Given a choice, you have to decide what will best suit your needs. If you have technique problems—particularly if you kick late, or ski flat-footed—you should not depend on skis that are easy to balance on, or ones that are slow and steady, because using these types will just compound your problem. On the other hand, if you ski well, or if you are just beginning, this type of roller ski would be O.K. If you need strength training, or a more powerful stride, you should not necessarily get the skis that are easy to move. (Although you can practice the diagonal stride on fairly steep sections of road and thus develop more strength this way.) And so on.

Of course a good way to check out advantages of various skis is to swap brands with someone else.

Some Tips on Beginning

I will list a few procedures that we have found useful.

1. In beginning to use roller skis, start with short sessions of 10 or 15 minutes three or four times a week. Get used to the skis and balance problems before you go off on longer trips. This may take a few weeks.

29 (near strip) **& 30** (frames in right strip). These vertical sequences demonstrate the close relationship between roller-skiing and x-c skiing. It's the same skier—and going at the same pace in both—training in early fall on a hardtopped road, and working out later on snow. Compare each left with each right frame to see the striking similarity of form throughout.

31 (strip far left) **& 32** (near strip). The vertical sequences opposite show two members of the U.S. Team—Tim Caldwell at left and Bill Koch at right—roller-skiing uphill. They're both using very strong, and similar, diagonal techniques, but there are subtle differences in style: in general, Bill's rear-arm and rear-leg carries are higher than Tim's, while Tim's are more classical. The point is, though, that individual styles are to be expected—and they're fine with me, as long as the basic technique is good, and totally efficient for each skier. (The actual pitch of the hill is shown best in the fourth shot from the top of each strip, by the way.)

2. Find roads that are smooth and that have a minimum of traffic.

3. Do most of your skiing on uphill sections. This is really the only place you can practice the diagonal technique. In fact, you can probably practice the diagonal on any hard-topped uphill section of road in North America. You can also practice the double-pole on easy uphill sections.

Use the flats for double-poling only, and don't use the downhills at all unless they are fairly gentle, smooth and have good runouts. Then you can coast down, or double-pole. It's easy to get out of control on a downhill. Flipping onto the pavement or the shoulder of the road is not as pleasurable as flipping into the snow during winter when you're on ski skis.

4. Get special carbide tips for your x-c poles if you use the roads.

Some companies have a couple of different tips that work well and do not wear out as fast as conventional pole tips. Or you can braze snow-tire studs on your own pole tips.

Binding Placement

Most skis are marked to show you where to put the bindings. Some skiers I know move their bindings so their feet are closer to the wheels that hold the ski from slipping, hoping to get better kick, or purchase. I think this is a mistake because, as I have already said, you tend to get spoiled and overconfident about your technique.

It's better to place the bindings at the recommended marks. If you do slip a bit now and then, analyze the reasons why. Probably you're skiing too flat-footed. Or kicking too hard. Different skiers react the same way to roller skis as they do to waxed skis. Some can handle almost any roller ski and not slip, while others have troubles with the same skis.

Advantages of Roller-skiing

It is the best form of specificity training you can do during the off-season. If the terrain is suitable and you can make a circuit beginning where you started—this means that the downhills aren't too steep, and that there are some uphills as well as flats—the demands on your system will be very similar to those of skiing a course, even though the techniques used in roller-skiing will not be exactly the same. (On roller skis you will double-pole the flats instead of using the diagonal, and probably coast the downhills instead of double-poling.)

By stressing roller-skiing uphill, using the diagonal technique, you can develop a stronger stride than you would otherwise on regular snow skiing.

Roller-skiing will prepare your muscles, particularly those in the groin area, for on-snow skiing. In this regard, when you start on snow you will be a week or two ahead of skiers who haven't done any roller-skiing. You will easily make the transfer to some good snow workouts right away.

Roller-skiing requires at bit more concentration than regular skiing in good tracks. It's easy for a roller ski to go askew and if one crosses in front of the other it can be very awkward! Some might list this as a disadvantage but, as before, I claim it's an advantage to have to concentrate on every stride. Good training!

There are no tracks to set, no skis to wax. (But you'd better oil the bearings once in a while, and keep all the screws and bolts tight. Did you ever lose a wheel while roller-skiing?)

Since roller-skiing technique has so many similarities with snow technique, you can take videotape pic-

tures of roller-skiing and analyze your problems. All this can be done during the long days of summer and fall, at a relaxed time, and when you won't have the standard winter problems of the video machine or operator freezing up.

And roller-skiing is a pretty good substitute for snow skiing during the competitive season if for some reason you can't get on snow.

Disadvantages

I've already hinted at the danger of injury. If you try going too fast too soon, or take some downhill sections you shouldn't, there is a danger of spraining an ankle or getting scraped up. One girl from our area wore the knees out of three pairs of sweatpants before she got accustomed to roller skis, and she was using them on just the flats. But hers is an extreme example.

Roller skis don't maneuver very well. Generally, you should avoid situations where turns are necessary. The step-around turn is the best way to change direction.

There have been some isolated cases of sore arms or elbows caused by the jarring of poles on the pavement. If you feel soreness, especially in the elbow joint, ease up on roller-skiing until you determine the cause. Then proceed accordingly.

Sometimes long downhills are too fast to roller-ski with safety and thus pose slight problems: how to get down them?—how to get home? Most skiers happily walk, jog or hitch-hike back. Some are in situations where they can actually depend on public transportation to bring them home. In Oslo, for instance, a skier can start downtown, take any number of routes that will eventually take him high above the fjord, then take a train or bus back.

And then there are the law-enforcement officials. In some areas roller skiers using the roads have been hauled in for operating without brakes, without lights, without license plates—you name it. But use good sense, the same considerations you'd use if you were hiking along the road. If need be, roller-ski facing oncoming traffic, just as you would in walking any road without a runners' or bikers' strip. Don't swing wide on blind curves; don't ski side by side on curves. Obey standard rules of pedestrian behavior on any road, especially a winding one.

Uphill Roller-skiing

The diagonal technique is used on all uphills and the length of the stride depends on the steepness of the hill. In any case, you can get quite a bit of power into your stride and thus develop good strength for skiing. A word of caution, however. Ratcheted wheels are like that super wax job that almost never slips. Under these conditions it's easy to begin to horse it too much—and if you do so your technique will begin to get rougher and rougher. Don't do it. Ease off and ski smoothly, correctly.

Some roller skis with a ratcheted front wheel will slip occasionally on the uphills. Sometimes the wheel may need tightening, but more often it's a problem with your skiing. If you don't have enough weight over the front wheel you won't get the necessary traction on it to help hold you from slipping. You can correct this slipping by getting more forward ankle-bend and by not trying to go quite so hard. It's just like skiing.

Roller-skiing the Flats

Double-poling is the best technique to use on the flats. You can make the motions exactly the same as you do on snow.

Occasionally, for a brush-up or review of your diagonal, you can cruise along on the flats with the single stride. It will be very easy, so if you aren't careful to go with a certain amount of smoothness, you'll get snarled up. But you can see how your rear ski is coming through or check how you are riding the front ski. Maybe this will require you to change the timing of your poling motion slightly, since you will glide longer in each stride. On the whole, though, it's very easy and relaxing to ski the flats.

Downhills

If you can roller-ski a downhill section I would recommend that you begin by standing up straight and relaxing. Occasionally the skis will wander a bit and you have to be ready to make small corrective steps to straighten them. This situation arises on snow too.

When you get good on the roller skis you can crouch or tuck and train the same downhill muscles you will use on snow. If you're skiing with someone else you will be able to see the advantage of a tuck over an upright stance that presents greater wind resistance.

If there's any question about your ability to negotiate a downhill on roller skis, take them off and walk. Be extra leery of curves.

8. Tempo & Speed Training

Speed and tempo workouts may be classified roughly under interval training. Some people consider them as the same, but I want to emphasize a distinction between the two.

Tempo training can be thought of as *pace-training at racing speed,* and it is usually done under steady-state conditions.

Speed training, by my definition, is an *all-out effort at maximum speed* —which, if continued long enough, would cause a person to go under.

A few examples will help clarify.

The most common tempo training is done by skiing at racing speeds on predominantly uphill terrain for periods of five minutes or more. This is a steady-state effort, and after it the skier usually takes a complete recovery before doing another run. (Usually, in interval training, the rest after each session is not complete; and also the speeds used in interval training vary.) The object of tempo training is to adjust the body to racing speeds and to learn to pace oneself.

There's no doubt that racers should go harder in the shorter races. If you go under in a sprint race, chances are you'll finish O.K.—though

---

Pace: Q.E.D.

The 1974 Holmenkollen 50-km race is a made-to-order example of the need for pacing in long-distance events. In important races like this, by the way, the interval times are calculated and broadcast to the crowds over radios and through the public-address system in the start-and-finish area. It was apropos the PA announcer's interim comments that Magne Myrmo, the winner, made an interesting observation on his performance.

Contrary to the broadcast announcements to the effect that he was gaining on everyone, especially during the last 10 k's of the circuit, he said this just wasn't so. His lap time for the first 25-km loop was within a few seconds of his time for the second lap. Thus he paced himself perfectly—and the others did not. Instead of his gaining on the field, he said, they all lost to him.

Nice summary.

probably not in the money. On the other hand, if you go under near the end of a 50-km race, you may have to be carried back to the finish. Moral: Pacing is more important in the long-distance events.

Speed training

Speed training can take many forms, but in general it consists of doing some skills at top speed for a very short period of time. My favorite off-season speed training is running 10–12-second uphill sprints (discussed in Chapter 9). I try to stress some of the features of the diagonal technique when doing this, especially coming off the ball of the foot and reaching forward with the hands.

In rowing you can do a "big ten" and go at it full force for those strokes. In roller-skiing you could either go at sprint speeds doing the double-pole, or the diagonal. And so on.

33. Start in 1979 of one wave of the classic 55-km Birkebeiner Race in Norway. Each skier must tote a 5-kg pack representing the weight of the infant Crown Prince Haakon, who was rescued and carried to safety by the Birkebeiner faction in 1206. "Birkebeiner" is Norwegian for "birch legs," and this tribe—noted for its skiing exploits—used birchbark much as we use gaiters today. Sweden's Vasaloppet is more widely publicized, but many racers consider the Birkebeiner more grueling because of the terrain and the backpack.

Plenty of uphill speed training can sure help in a scramble like this one!

There is some controversy about the value of skiing at top speeds, speeds so fast that your technique may begin to break down. But I firmly believe it is important to do ski sprints of 100–200 meters occasionally. This will train the body to be able to ski faster, and eventually skiing at racing speeds will seem easier. I have seen a lot of relay races lost on the home stretch because the anchor man couldn't ski fast enough. This is reason enough for speed training.

Just pick out a good track, perhaps slightly uphill, be sure you are warmed up—and then go. I mean, really go at it! We've had match races for 150 meters at Putney that have left the track pulverized and the air full of snow from the thrashing given it by the racers.

Speed training has spin-off value as a strength-builder too. To put your muscles under stress in a high-speed situation is so taxing that I list some of these speed sessions as strength workouts.

Bicycle Bumps

Another variation for speed and strength training is practicing on "bicycle bumps." Shovel a series of mounds of snow of varying heights and at varying distances, pack them so they are smooth enough to ski over and put in a track. Then shave down the left track on the first bump, the right track on the second bump, and so on: the idea is to have the opposing tracks at different heights. You may have to water the snow slightly to help it set up firmly. When you ski into the first bump with a little speed you'll find that the track forces your legs to simulate the full pedaling motion of a bicycle rider. If the bumps are spaced close enough you should be able to accelerate even without poling. The different spacing between bumps offers syncopation that does wonders for your timing, especially at high speeds. A track of about 100 meters, full of these bumps, can provide a very strenuous and sometimes amusing ride. (Shoveling the snow is a bonus strength workout too.)

9. Strength Training

The various kinds of strength training remind me of long skirts—they come and go with the passing of the years. At this writing, many coaches and skiers in the United States are on an upswing with weight-lifting while other countries are avoiding it. Most of the weight-lifting programs I am familiar with in this country have been adopted on general principles rather than on the results of tests for efficacy: I know of no scientific study of weight-lifting programs for skiers.

The different kinds of strength training

There is no question of the value of strength for the x-c skier. And it's not enough to be strong; you must be able to use that strength with a certain amount of speed. This strength-speed combination is referred to as your power. You might be able to do certain strength-building exercises under tremendous loads at slow speeds, but unless you can transform this ability to a movement with faster speed—and specifically a movement used in x-c skiing—your strength will be of little avail.

The most common type of strength training is lifting weights. Done correctly, this sort of training develops the muscles used in the particular lifts you are performing.

Another type of strength training consists of doing ski movements against resistance. The object here is to develop the same muscles used in skiing. Roller-skiing and pulling on armbands are two examples of this kind of exercise (both described in Chapter 7, on specificity).

A third kind of training is what I call over-all, co-ordinated strength training, which fosters the ability to use muscle groups from various parts of your body in harmonious effort. Weight-lifting and ski-movements-against-resistance will not necessarily develop this skill. I'm sure you have seen many a strong person who could not use his strength in a co-ordinated way, and many a co-ordinated person who had no strength to use: neither has what I define as co-ordinated strength.

It's this kind of over-all strength that really separates x-c skiing from distance foot-running—and the sheep from the goats. A good skier must be able to use so many different muscles in skiing uphill, around corners, over bumps, through poor tracks, on bad wax, downhill, etc., that learning one set of concerted movements by roller-skiing alone, for instance, is not enough. There's always some new situation to cope with in x-c skiing. You might be off balance, you might have just slipped on one ski, your pole may have missed its mark, and so on. I'll say more about this later.

Areas of agreement

It's generally agreed that strength-building programs should be progressive and should be done at stress loads.

A schedule of strength training three times a week, with at least a day off between each session, is indicated.

During the competitive season you can probably keep your strength level by training two days a week. It should not be necessary to try and progress during the season.

There is probably a high correlation between strength and muscular endurance. However, there is not full agreement on the relationship between increasing one aspect by training for the other. For example, do

34. Wrestling 4-foot sections of hardwood over to a pile makes the felling seem like a piece of cake.

heavy loads with few repetitions, as in the case of weight-lifting, build muscular endurance?—or should it be lesser loads with many repetitions?

The *Pro's* of Weight-lifting

There is a lot of literature about weight-lifting and I am not going to get into detailed descriptions of various programs here. Lack of space prohibits it and, as you might have guessed, I prefer other approaches to strength training.

The advantages of weight-lifting are as follows:

It can be made progressive. The weights are easily measured and adjusted. The results are easily seen and therefore are gratifying.

Special muscle groups can be developed by weight-lifting. This is particularly advantageous for patients recovering from injuries or surgery. I have had firsthand experience with this and there is no doubt in my mind that for rehabilitation after certain injuries, weight-lifting is the best method.

The *Con's* of Weight-lifting

Some of the disadvantages of weight-lifting are:

There is a chance of developing some muscles you don't need for x-c skiing; in fact, if weight programs are not done correctly there is some danger of losing flexibility and gaining too much weight at the same time.

Lifting weights can be dreary work.

You can't take weights with you everywhere, and if you are going to continue strength work during the competitive season you may have to develop another program for yourself.

Finally, some experiments indicate that the VO_2 uptake in muscles developed by weight-lifting is not as great as in muscles developed by endurance training.

Instead of barbells

I have to put in a plug for logging since I live in the country. I use the term logging to include cutting brush, cutting and splitting firewood, and hauling it to my stoves and the sauna.

In the 1950's and early '60's several of the world's top skiers were loggers and many aspiring x-c'ers believed that in order to win races you had to be a logger. Then many skiers, particularly in the United States, went through a period of more sophisticated weight training, using everything from homemade devices to Nautilus machines. But now, with the energy crunch, the emphasis on wood-cutting has returned, at least in my section of the country. Yippee!

You show me a skier who has been doing a lot of logging and I'll show you a guy—the same person—who is really strong and who will be able to use his strength better than the person who has been lifting weights.

You might wonder how logging can be made progressive, according to the established rules for strength-training. It's actually pretty simple. You go out and thrash around the brush, clear it, cut your trees, limb them, section them, split them, throw them into a pile and pick them up—oh, you're tired? Your legs, arms and back ache? O.K. Knock it off for the day.

Come back again another day and continue. Keep it up. Then after a few weeks, if you think you aren't progressing, get one of your friends out there with you and ask him to pitch in, and see how long he lasts. Or compare the volume of wood you last cut with the first product of the few days you were out.

Actually, it isn't hard to measure your progress. You can just tell when you've had a good workout.

This co-ordinated strength approach is very interesting. I give the example of a couple of boys who were training for skiing. They occasionally attended training camps where they were tested in such things as the bench press. One boy did a fair amount of rowing one spring, following the ski season, and without lifting weights since November, showed up in June and pressed 20 pounds more than he had in the fall. Another one, doing a lot of brush cutting and "piddling" work like that, raised his bench-press maximum by 20 pounds in a period of two months, again without lifting weights formally.

Maybe rowing and logging (or cutting brush) do increase your ability to lift heavier weights. The interesting question follows: Does weight-lifting increase your ability to log or row? How transferable is the strength gained by weight-lifting?

Logging—marvelous work. It's outside, in natural surroundings; and, as we say in Vermont, "The person who cuts his own wood gets warmed by it twice."

Ski motions against resistance

Too many strength-building programs, especially weight-lifting ones, stress the development of the upper body, the arms and shoulders.

There are two problems with this approach. For one, the strength gained by lifting weights is not necessarily transferable to skiing. For the other, programs of this sort slight the use of the legs.

But you ski with your legs, with most of your skiing strength coming from well below your shoulders. Therefore you should train your legs and lower body. I have already described such specificity exercises as roller-skiing, ski-bounding and ski-striding. In addition, there are several valuable exercises that use extra resistance to build strength—for skiing.

CPT 8: You should train the muscles that will be used in skiing and, as much as possible, train them by using the same movements that are used in skiing.

Running in Water

This is very good for leg-lifting strength, quite similar to that used in skiing uphill. An ocean beach is the best place for it, because you can intersperse running in thigh-deep water with sprints along the

35 (near strip) **& 36** (opposite strip). These vertical sequences offer fascinating similarities between running in thigh-deep water and skiing uphill. Rolf Kjaernsli, Norwegian coach, regarded his romp in Long Island Sound as a training exercise; Oddvar Braa of Norway, 1979 World Cup winner, is the skier.

Leg Workouts

shore, following the waves' high-water mark as they roll over the beach in uneven patterns. If you feel the workout isn't tough enough get into deeper water and then run up a few sand dunes for variety.

Be aware of blisters that may develop on your feet from running barefooted. Running in old shoes or sneakers is out, since they fill with sand and become quite uncomfortable.

Legbands

Using legbands—a logical variation on armbands—is a good exercise for developing forward knee-drive. In

37. New idea for those shot bicycle inner-tubes called "Putney armbands": use 'em as legbands.

working with legbands be sure not to initiate the forward leg-drive with a slight swing from the hip, because doing so could lead to bad x-c technique habits.

The *foot* should lead the power stroke forward, in a pendulum motion, and then the rest of the leg, from the lower part up, joins in the effort. This happens very fast and it is quite a subtle movement which may be hard to discern.

Hill Sprints

This is a good anaerobic exercise to build strength and speed, which combine to form power. There may be some other value as an anaerobic exercise which has yet to be determined.

The best approach is to get warmed up, then run sprints up a hill for 10–12 seconds. Go just as fast as you can! If you walk back down you should be ready to start again when you get to the bottom. Try to maintain good forward-body position and come off the ball of your foot with each step (rather than leaning back slightly and running flat-footed, as you would if you ran slowly): if you think about slanting your whole body forward it might help. Make a conscious effort to reach ahead with the arms and not just run with them tight or making very small arcs.

In time you can work up to 15 or 20 of these, quite easily.

Sit-ups, Back-ups

Sit-ups and back-ups are very good strengtheners for the abdominal and back muscles.

You all know what sit-ups are like and how they are done. The best ones are done with bent knees and with your feet anchored by a strap or by someone holding them down. After you get fairly proficient at these you can make them more effective (difficult, too) by holding some weights on your head. Then, the next degree of difficulty involves doing them on an incline, with your head low of course.

Back-ups feel more restrictive because you just can't bend as easily or as far when you're lying on your stomach. But put your hands behind your head, get some means of anchoring your feet or ankles, and lift up legs straight this time. When it gets easy, hold some weights on your head. Continue.

Finally, if you're feeling really tough, do them on an incline with your head low again.

Pull-ups, Dips

Pull-ups (also called "chinning")

38 (frames at left) **& 39** (above).   Martha Rockwell does her sit-ups with a 10-pound weight for overload, and with feet anchored; the pillow protects her coccyx, and flexed knees prevent the wrong kind of strain on her lower back. Her back-ups in the strip above strengthen the muscles so vital in maintaining a strong single stride in racing (components of the stride are described at length in Chapter 16).

are a stand-by whose virtues are well known for arm and shoulder work.

A recent addition to many skiers' repertory is the dip, in which the skier does a sort of inside-out push-up from behind—if you follow me. The muscles used in lifting the body are the same ones as those used in

41 (below). No Olympic grant-money needed for this dip machine: it's two sugar-maple saplings nailed about 2 feet apart like a gymnast's parallel bars. The skier has fairly strong arms and can do her dips in this position, but beginners often need to support some of their weight by hooking their heels over the saplings so that their legs are nearly at right angles to the torso. Later, as they get stronger, they can let their legs dangle, using only arms and shoulders to raise and lower the full body weight.

40. Strong arm and shoulder-girdle muscles mean strong poling action (again, see Chapter 16), so Martha does pull-ups—also called "chinning."

the most vigorous poling, thus making dips the single most valuable exercise of the four shown right here.

Toe Rises

Stand a little less than a meter from a wall, lean on the wall by placing your hands slightly above your head height, then while keeping your butt and your head parallel to the wall, do toe rises. When this gets easy start over again with two legs but wear a weighted pack. Then shift to one leg. And so on.

As usual, the technique here is important. If you rush ahead too fast with your weights, or by getting onto one leg too soon, you may end up doing toe rises off a flat foot, or by initiating the action with a little twitch of the abdomen. The point is to strengthen the foot, ankle and lower leg muscles, so these are the

42. Strength work can include carrying broken-down snowmobiles out of the woods after snow melts in the spring. With the driver aboard the task can be made more challenging.

main muscles you should use. When you come down your weight should be on the forward part of your foot and you can actually do a slight kneebend before going up again into another toe rise.

In sum: All these ski movements against resistance are probably more enjoyable than standard weight-lifting. I think they are better. But they have one disadvantage and that is this: these exercises are sometimes hard to measure for progress. The best way to discover your progress is by keeping a descriptive training journal, the log I talked about in Chapter 4.

Work on the Weak Link

Many of the younger athletes I train complain occasionally about some part of their anatomy giving out during a training session or a race. I tell them that everyone has a weak link and that usually, when you go hard, something will give. If it didn't, we'd all be Olympic champions.

Recently I've seen more backs "torn apart" during the fall and winter than seems necessary. I think many more athletes are training harder and getting stronger. In particular, they are doing a fantastic job of building their leg and upper-body strength. But their lower-back and abdominal muscles have not been trained in concert with the rest of the body and therefore these muscles are suffering from the strain that is sometimes placed on them. It's almost always the back that gives out when you do any excessive amount of hard work, so heed the warning and train your back muscles.

10. Inseason Training

While offseason training may take place for as much as eight months out of the year—and therefore is considered more important than inseason workouts—it's the inseason training that is the most delicate and difficult to plan.

Here is the place for individual differences. Here is the place for each skier to apply his hard-won knowledge of himself, of his strengths and weaknesses and reactions, and to keep in mind what he learned from keeping his training log (Chapter 4). This is no time for commonly accepted routines, which, if imposed now, perhaps could be responsible for erratic racing results.

The schedules I propose below are based on several points, or beliefs, that I will go into first.

Some of the dangers

I've seen too many skiers take to snow in the beginning of the season and never do any more foot-running or strength work. As the season goes on, they lose part of their pulmonary (breathing) capacity; they lose some of their strength; and finally, they lose some of their speed—all conditions that were probably at higher levels at the very beginning of the season.

Most of the coaches and athletes I've talked with admit that they should continue with some sort of foot-running and strength program during the competitive season, but they just slide into a routine of all skiing and then begin to suffer a deconditioning effect.

Traveling, or Training?

Travel plus an intensive race schedule can practically ruin a skier in a matter of a few weeks. Suppose you have a race coming up which requires some travel; you rest up and travel, then race. Next thing you know, it's time to travel again to the next race. Meanwhile the food is different, you're in different sleeping situations every night or two, and after a while you begin to wonder what happened to your training program. Well, it went out the window when you first took on a schedule requiring you to travel and race so often.

"Training" Races

You should spend a great deal of time in planning an intelligent schedule for the whole winter, with emphasis on just certain, important races. The other races should be counted by you, in your own mind, as training races or progress races.

For instance, in the beginning of the season you might travel to your first race, knowing you haven't had much skiing. It's rather pointless, under the circumstances, to put a lot of value on your results in this one. Furthermore, you might be better off to plan your day so you could race and then take another spin around the track in order to get in some extra kilometers. Your plan might even call for arriving at the race site a day early and getting in a good workout, one much more intensive than you would normally take before a race day.

If you are committed to some awkward schedule of travel and racing you must try to make the best of it. This might mean taking a good run at the airport; or if in the city, at some park far removed from the ski scene. This isn't so bad, and in fact it fits in with my recommended schedule.

A minimum schedule

It's generally agreed that three good cardiovascular workouts a week will be ample to keep that system at its present level. For strength, probably two workouts a week will suffice to maintain level. So here are a couple of minimums to take into account during the winter season.

The cardiovascular workouts would usually be accomplished by skiing. Practice during the week is one example. Certainly a race would qualify as a workout of this type.

Instead of Weights

If you've been on weights all year you might find yourself in a situation without weights. (Can't you see the fellow at the airlines counter lifting your box of weights onto the conveyor belt—and then figuring the excess-luggage fee?) The alternative is other kinds of strength work. We've tried all sorts of ideas and most of them have merit.

The Exergenie is a marvelously versatile device for carrying along on any trip. As noted earlier, you can set it up practically anywhere.

If you like the out-of-doors you may find yourself in a situation where you can go chop wood or shovel snow. Or you can go out with one of your buddies and take turns carrying each other piggyback.

A Minimum Schedule

You should find situations where you can do some of your regular strength work at least twice a week. It doesn't take long.

In addition, you should continue with your sit-ups and back-ups on a regular basis. Many skiers recently have been plagued with back problems during the season and I find that most of them had stopped doing all their back exercises once they got on snow. After a while, something is likely to give, and if it's your back that fails, then you are in deep trouble.

Some Foot-running

I would include two days of foot-running every week. This should be rather short and intensive, maybe only 15–20 minutes, of course after a good warm-up. The foot-running offers several advantages. By going at it hard you will keep your breathing capacity up. I've always found that I breathed harder foot-running than skiing. (Maybe it's because I didn't know how to run, you say? Doesn't matter, it's good conditioning.) Also, it helps to keep your speed of movement high if you run hard.

Finally, it's assumed that at the beginning of the snow season you came off a program of running. To continue twice a week, even running fairly hard, is just a drop in the bucket, and if you keep it up during the season, come spring you will find yourself a week or two ahead of the fellow who doesn't run during the winter. I might also mention that sometimes you will be forced to run, maybe even longer distances, in order to get a work-out. You might be traveling, or weathered out, or living too far from snow to ski every day. Then running (or roller-skiing) is a must.

Rest Days

There are rest days and there are rest days. What might seem to be a very imposing workout for you will be considered a rest day for another.

Most top skiers in the world take some exercise every day of the week. The easier days are called rest days, or active rest days, and they consist of easy, no-strain skiing, or an easy jog of some sort. Even during travel most athletes get in a bit of exercise, maybe just enough to break a sweat.

If you aren't sick, you should exercise every day. Keep the motor tuned up. Besides, you never know what the next day will bring. It's possible you won't be able to train, for some reason. A bird in the hand . . .

Other skiers prefer to simplify matters during the season and they "tour" about 25–35 km a day for training, then take it easy the day before a competition. Otherwise, they rest and skip strength work and foot-running.

In sum: As a minimum during the competitive season I recommend for each week two days of foot-running and three other cardiovascular work-outs (preferably skiing), and two days of strength work.

Head Problems, Peaking & Psyching

A popular phrase used these days to explain a racer's poor results is that he has "a head problem." The implication is that he has the necessary background training, the skills, the support in terms of good equipment, waxing and coaching, but just can't get it together.

The so-called head problems may be another name for being off peak. Racers who are really doing well during any part of the season, or who have peaked, are not accused of having head problems. Are we to suppose, then, if these same racers do not perform so well during other parts of the season, that they are simply having head problems? Not likely. It's probably a matter of being off peak.

How peaking works

We've all heard about peaking; it's something lots of skiers can talk about yet seem rather helpless in planning for. The successful athletes are able to be at top form for the big races, and we say of them that they have peaked, or are "at peak." Occasionally an athlete goes through the whole year at top form, but such an optimum is fairly rare. Whether this is because the season is too long for most skiers to operate at peak, or because so few know how to stay at peak, is another ongoing argument.

But it still gets back to the more important notion and that is this: An athlete must know himself well enough to plan his own training and competitive schedule. A top Swedish skier, S. A. Lundbeck, won a race in December of the 1977–78 season and was disturbed at having done so well. He wanted to peak during the FIS later in February, and was afraid he could not hold his present form from December until then. So he withdrew from all competition for a few weeks and started in with more distance training. This was followed by another build-up in intensity at the end of that period just before the FIS. His results at the FIS? Two gold medals and two sixth-place finishes in four races. Rather commendable, to say the least. He knew himself.

The most famous example of peaking involves Lasse Viren, the Finnish foot-runner. Viren has won gold medals in the 1972 and 1976 Olympics but has enjoyed a reputation as an also-ran in virtually all his other im-

43. Vermont version of a late season strength workout: gathering maple sap in the sugarbush. Many U.S. Team members have been brought to their knees by a day of such sidehill work in old corn snow

portant competitions. In 1972, just before the Olympic Games, I attended the yearly track and field meet between Sweden and Finland. Viren was not present to run for his country. The understanding fans told me that he was working on peaking for the Games at Munich a few weeks hence; therefore the events at Helsinki represented a rather unimportant meet. Well, peak he did at Munich, winning two golds.

Viren disappeared from prominence for a few years, and, as more of you may remember, came back in Montreal in 1976 for two more golds. At that time he said he would be back in 1980. We'll see about that one. But nonetheless his Olympic performances were astounding, apparently perfectly planned and executed.

This peaking idea is not restricted to one skier or athlete during one part of a season, but can be approached on a much broader scale. In 1978 the Finnish Ski Team was very successful in the FIS, finishing second only to the Russians. During the 1979 season they were a bust—a result not surprising to them, or to others familiar with their program. The Finns are on record as liking to point for the FIS and the Olympic Games. These events occur during the even-numbered years, and at this writing I feel that no one should expect big results from the Finns in the odd years.

Ways to Reach Peak

Cross-country ski racers are continually faced with planning problems. It's one thing to try to peak for some selection races for a place on the team, often held early in the season. It's another thing to plan for a long series of races, like the World Cup schedule which, in the 1979 season, began before Christmas 1978 and lasted through early March. Throw in the National Championships, some favorite local races, even some divisional championships, and you can begin to appreciate the difficulty. Add to all of this the pressures from coaches, clubs, schools, friends, family, the press, and you may begin to get a real head problem.

Seriously now, I have seen three slightly different approaches to peaking and I put them forth here. Each may have advantages. Each may be less important than a skier's own program or confidence in his own ability. But here goes.

Plan 1. Skiers work hard to peak a few weeks before the big event, let's say one like the Olympic Games, which last for 10 days. They basically change over from a lot of distance work to doing more and more interval and speed work. They try to get near peak form during the last few races that occur several days, perhaps two weeks, before the Games. From then on they try to hold form by skiing easy distance every day, but taper off slightly a day or two before the big competition.

Plan 2. Skiers try to peak as in Plan 1. But instead of daily doses of easy distance work, they work fairly hard for 3 to 4 days and then allow at least 2 days of nearly complete rest before the competition.

Plan 3. Skiers try to peak several days before their major events by very hard workouts running a tough series of less important races. They actually spend more time on intervals and speed work than on Plans 1 and 2. The peak is followed by several days' rest, perhaps as many as 5 to 7. Then they enter their big events.

Plans 1 and 2 may differ only according to an individual's taste, but no one can be sure; I think I would lean toward Plan 2. On the other hand,

Plan 3 may lend itself to something like the Olympics, but I would not be surprised to find a general falling-off after that. This is based on the following conjecture of mine.

Conjecture: In skiing, the duration of work (or, roughly, the distance skied) and the speed of work (the speed you ski) are inversely related—the faster you ski the less far you can go.

Well, that seems obvious to everyone, I guess. But there is a drastic falling-off of the duration factor in this little formula if a lot of high speed—i.e., racing—is engaged in. It's not a case of the skier operating in a nice balance by running a few races and doing some distance work. If he does too much high-speed skiing, the skier either will not be able to ski enough distance to keep in good shape, or else in doing so his effort will be counterproductive and he will probably get tired or sick.

Training effects like muscle hypertrophy, enhancement of enzymatic conversion of food to energy, and enhancement of the oxygen-transport system are best achieved with duration of work as the dominant contributing factor, although it's fairly certain that the rate or speed of work is also important.

Thus a skier who enters several small races during a short period of time is apt to come out on the short end of the duration factor. In Plan 3, with a maximum of four races in a 10-day period like the Olympics, and with several days' rest before the meet and during the meet itself, a skier will probably suffer later on in the season from a loss of training effects. But if he had top results in the Games he can be content.

In sum: Plans 1 and 2 are the most conservative and the skier who follows one of these will probably have some good results during the season. He may not be able to predict his finishes accurately, however.

Peaking is fraught with variations, theories, even superstition. Many coaches have their pet theories, but too few racers have plans for themselves. Once again, the individual is the key, and you are best advised to try different routines yourself until you find one that works. Be sure to keep track of them in your training log.

Aggressive skiing

Skiers approach competition with different attitudes, so anything that can be done to encourage a racer to think positively and aggressively should be encouraged.

I've known racers who have been nearly sick at the thought of some long uphills, or fast downhills; or who have worried about a long piece of flat across a lake or pond. Coaches should try to forestall these situations, and here are a couple of different tactics.

First, get the racer thinking in terms of his strengths. Let's say he is strong on uphills. Then the coach will tell him he is going to make time here, that he should look forward to certain hills with the expectation of passing people, and so on.

Next, the coach should train the racers to think in terms of gaining time on little sections like corners, short uphills, short downhills, bumps, etc. Have practice on these sections by skiing the approaches to them, the sections themselves, and then the parts right after them. Analyze the fastest techniques, try the sections over and over until the skiers have them mastered. Then remind them before the race to ski those sections just the way they did in practice.

If racers are continually looking forward to sections of the course, and if they are thinking in terms of gaining time on them, chances are their results will be better than if they just go and ski hard, or "Go for it!"

Psyching

One of the popular terms nowadays is *psyched* or *psyching*, used as "psyched up" to denote a competitor's win-or-bust frame of mind; or, conversely, as "psyched out" to describe a defeatist attitude induced by any number of factors.

Psyching exists in x-c racing even though the practice is nowhere near so intense as the much-publicized measures attributed to Muhammad Ali before a championship fight or to certain linebackers before a Super Bowl. Actually, since the average x-c racer is not much like your average boxer or linebacker, the psyching bit is not so standard and does not even have the expected results in all cases. I've talked to a lot of racers who go all to pieces when they get psyched, or when coaches and spectators try to get them psyched: They get nervous, start too fast, flounder around on the course, often quit.

On the other hand, some skiers do get psyched and this happens in different ways.

Psyching

Some skiers can actually get themselves psyched, and this is fine for them; they are the lucky ones. Other skiers get psyched, sometimes by accident. Something might happen at the breakfast table or on the way to the race that morning that will start things off. From there it's all peaches and cream and the racer is "wired" all day.

Some coaches have methods that work with certain athletes, these ploys being invoked for the big races. It might be some goofy chant, or joke, or even serious discussion. It could be just a pep talk to serve as a confidence-builder. There are as many approaches as the product of the number of coaches multiplied by the number of racers. And that's a lot.

So there is no pat formula. But isn't it grand to have a few unpredictables? It makes everything more interesting.

11. Diet & the Supplements Debate

Just as soon as North American skiers got back into x-c after World War II they started coming in with food fads. I remember some of our racers' taking blueberry juice and wheat germ at every meal; in fact, they were rarely seen without a bottle of the mixture, which they valued as highly as their wax kits. Later in the 1950's buttermilk made a good run with some racers, although it never quite measured up to the blueberry potion in popularity.

During the '60's articles began appearing, especially from abroad, that vouched for the wonders of vitamin supplements. The Russians came in with a pitch for Vitamin E. Nearly everyone made a plug for at least one of the B-complex materials. Meanwhile, the coaches and racers were busily trying to keep abreast of the latest developments.

Now that the 1980's are upon us the pitch for vitamins has died a bit, but carbohydrate-loading is more popular than ever. At the same time, studies are being made on utilization of fats, and maybe someday we will be trying fat-loading. Who knows?

If you want to rest easy, be assured that if your diet is normal and well balanced, you will be getting all the food and vitamins you need. It's normal to expect growing kids to want more food, or for athletes who exercise a great deal to want more food. So if your diet is balanced and you aren't gaining weight, chances are very good that it's O.K.

Two warnings

The first: If you think that some year-round special diet or vitamin supplement is going to improve your performance, you are almost certainly wrong. There is no strong evidence to warrant this assumption.

The second: If you begin to depend on an overbalance of special foods or on vitamins for improved performances you are probably over the hill. I have seen some veteran skiers turn to this approach during the twilight of their careers.

CPT 9: You improve your performance through your training and technique programs, not through your eating and pill programs.

The *Con's* and *Pro's* of Supplements

Now I'm going to backtrack slightly.

Taking many of these extra foods and vitamin pills probably will not hurt you if they are taken in proper amounts; they probably will not help you either, in a pure physical sense. But they might help you psychologically. So if you think you can't get along without, say, your vitamin supplements, it would be a good idea to check with your doctor to make sure that the dose you are taking is actually not harmful, and that the vitamins contain nothing that might show up in a drug test.

Apropos the latter, in the doping-control tests being given after races now, certain vitamin supplements, because of some of the additives they contain, will produce positive results. Of course the intent of the doping test is not to disqualify an athlete for taking vitamins: the test is so sensitive that it picks up the additives, whose mere presence is enough to register Positive, no question of degree.

However, almost all the doctors I have talked with around the world think that vitamin supplements may have an influence in preventing disease among athletes, particularly those who travel away from their own environments. Therefore many team doctors I know prescribe vitamin pills for their skiers. But, to repeat, these are not given with the intention of improving performance. The doctors hope they are *preventive* in regard to catching colds, or getting some other sickness.

There are certain adjustments in the diet that can be made during the pre-race days, and on race days. I will say more about these in a minute.

Doping

I have never been associated with anyone who has taken pep pills or anything else like them in order to try to improve his performance during a race. There was quite a bit of speculation during the FIS meet in 1970 about one country's skiers who were alleged to be taking dope. This was never proven, and I think they were just skiing better than anyone expected them to; in fact, they kept winning for the rest of the season—and this indicates they were *not* on dope.

Since 1970 the Fédération Internationale de Ski has provided for more and more doping controls. Now after World championship events, the top three finishers, and other skiers picked at random, are subjected to doping tests to see if they have used any form of illegal stimulant. You can occasionally read about doping of athletes, or countries who have perfected some drug that will not show up in a doping test, but I think x-c skiing is clean so far. Every doping test on an x-c skier I know of has proven to be negative.

Pills

No paper or account I know of certifies to the advantage of taking some form of pep pill or dope. In fact, the studies show the adverse effects and indicate clearly that this is an area to avoid. Most of the drugs stimulate the heart to excessively high rates which could lead to dangerous situations such as damage to the heart or even death. The invulnerability-of-the-heart theory goes out the window under stimulation by drugs. Unfortunately, some athletes in other sports have died, apparently from a result of drug usage during competitions.

The most important argument, really, against any form of doping is a philosophical one. An x-c race is a contest between individuals to compare their strengths in endurance, technique, motivation and even waxing ability. You can think of all these as skills gained through training. It's a highly individual event: it's *you,* how *you* can perform, utilizing the skills you have developed during your training program. To bring in elements in the form of pharmacology or medical aid (if I can call doping that—in the medical profession they're called "interventions"), or elements not natural to the body, is contrary to the whole idea of competition.

Or look at it this way. Suppose a vote was taken among sportsmen regarding the use of drugs. Do you think they would vote in favor of the idea?

If there are some elements connected with the sporting world who want to use dope for one reason or another, perhaps they should have their own events, no holds barred. I wouldn't even be interested in hearing the results.

Blood-doping

There's another interesting approach to improving performance that involves doctoring the athlete's blood. Many weeks before a competitive event an athlete gives up a certain amount of blood; it is centrifuged, and the plasma, containing mostly RBC (red blood cells), is stored in a blood bank. Meanwhile the athlete starts in on his training program again and rebuilds his own blood supply. Then, a short time before the big race the athlete is given back his own blood, thus significantly increasing his RBC and hemoglobin count, and therefore increasing his O_2 transport facility.

The proponents of this method argue that it's the athlete's own blood, isn't it? And so on.

Well, the more the athlete depends on medical teams, or things like blood-doping, in order to improve his performance, the more we will be taking something away from him and from the meaning of his training and racing. Soon he will begin to wonder whose race it is.

Blood-doping is difficult to detect and the rules are not clear regarding its legality. Most countries have an unwritten understanding that they will not resort to this tactic, for reasons of sport.

Pre-race diet

There is a training-eating schedule used by thousands of athletes for a number of years and there seems to be more and more evidence to show that it is effective. Essentially, two or three days before the race the athlete takes a long workout, one hard enough to deplete the glycogen stores in the body. Then he feeds himself primarily on carbohydrates from that time until the race. It has been found that using this regime will actually build the glycogen stores to a higher level than existed before.

Some bikers I know go a step further and take a week of protein diet, then a tough workout which really depletes the glycogen, and then they go onto the carbohydrates for several days preceding the race.

The most important thing to remember about pre-racing eating is that you should not experiment during the big races. Work out a system for yourself during training sessions much earlier in the year, then hold with it during the race season.

Race-day food

Since carbohydrates are easily digested and readily utilized for energy it is a good idea to continue eating "carbos" on the day of the race. There is room for quite a bit of personal preference here with regard to the timing of the last meal before the race, and the content of the meal. Naturally, about everything has been tried, and most athletes like to eat about three hours before the event.

This is an item you should keep track of in your training log. Don't be alarmed if you have some of your best days, or workouts, shortly after a meal consisting largely of fats and proteins. That's O.K.; others have had this experience. On the other hand, some athletes have very definite needs for restricting the food they take in before a race.

Time Out

During distance training or long-distance competitions the break provided by feeding is almost always welcomed by the athlete. Nevertheless there is that danger of losing one's concentration right after the feed, and in a race this usually means a slowing in speed. I love those feeds myself, and if someone else—like another athlete training with me, another racer arriving at the food station, or a coach standing there yelling at me—wasn't around I might just linger and have seconds and thirds. But even if one "double-feeds" as some racers do, it's important to get one's mind, as well as those skis, back on the track.

44. Ernie Lennie of the Canadian National Ski Team feeds during the North American Championships' 30-km race in March 1975.

Liquids During the Race

The liquid balance in the body is very important. Before a race you should drink a normal amount of whatever you prefer. Don't sell yourself short—but don't stock up, either, in anticipation of heavy sweating. If the race is over 15 km, or if you are going to "feed" (take in liquids) along the way, I think it is a good idea to begin your feeding a few minutes before you start. This certainly is something you should practice during your longer workouts so you can learn your body's preferences in feeding.

The whole idea of feeding during a race is to supply some energy and liquids to replace those you burn up. It's highly probable that none of the top racers in the world could finish a long-distance event like the 50 km at a pace consistent with good performance without feeding during the race. The amount and content of the drink is another subject for long discussions around the potbelly stove. Before we knew any better, we used to take straight honey during a race. This did not provide liquid enough—in fact, in order to digest honey the stomach calls on liquid from other parts of the body—so we ended up thirstier than before. The honey also provided more energy than we could possibly utilize in a short time.

So a few guides are important. Since a person can absorb only about 50 grams of glucose an hour, and only about 4/5 liter of liquid an hour, it does no good to exceed these limits during feeding. If your stomach is bloated (the doctors call it "gastric overfilling"!) you'll be uncomfortable, and your reaction might impair your ability to ski at an optimum pace.

Some theories hold that fruit juices, especially ones containing citric acid, are bad for the stomach during competition and therefore should be avoided. However, I have always had pretty good luck with a touch of lemon juice in a mixture of tea and dextrose. The acid juice helps cut through that mucky feeling in the mouth.

The old, standard drink of coffee with sugar wasn't far off the mark either. If you believe in replacing some of the minerals in the body—which is one of the features of commercial drinks like Sportade and Gatorade—and get a feeling of being stimulated by the caffeine, you might prefer this.

Sometimes I add a little salt, just enough to be noticeable but not unpleasant when tasting the drink before the race. Then, during the race, the added salt actually tastes good.

Feeding every 15 minutes during the race seems to be indicated. At this rate, and remembering the body's capacity for absorption, you should try to feed a little less than 6 ounces a stop. Actually, this is quite a mouthful.

111

12. Altitude Training

In 1964, soon after the 1968 Olympic Summer Games were awarded to Mexico City (which has an altitude of about 2300 m), physiologists earnestly began studying the effects of athletic performances and training at higher altitudes. Now, more than a decade later, altitude training is still quite a controversial subject. (CPT 1 again: but who expects unanimity?)

With some fear and trepidation I make the following introductory statements, hoping there is little argument about them. From there we can go on.

1. For endurance events you can expect weaker or slower performances at high altitudes from around 1600 m and up, as compared to sea level. And you get them. For standard running distances there is a marked increase in times at altitude, and it is quite close to a linear relationship. At 2000 m the running times for distances will be off on the order of 7 percent; at 3000 m, 10 percent; and at 4500 m they will be off by about 20 percent.

2. A lowlander on arriving at altitude should go out deliberately to experience going under by doing a few sprints. Then he should see what happens when he tries either to recover, or to continue at what he considers a reasonable pace at sea level. If he practices this routine a few times he will probably not only learn something about pacing, but also he may not suffer the sensation of going under during a race. Mark this well: If a skier goes under in a race at altitude, he will have a tough time recovering.

3. The basic reason for decreased performances at altitude is that the air pressure is lower and therefore the body cannot take in so much O_2 to utilize in the production of energy.

4. The FIS—the world governing body of skiing—rules state in principle that world championship events in x-c skiing cannot be held on a course any part of which is above 1650 m. The generally stated reason for this rule is that since the lowland athletes would need so much time to acclimatize themselves to altitude the expenses would be prohibitive. Probably another reason the rule went in was that the lowland countries felt they might be at a disadvantage, physically and psychologically, if they had to run at altitude.

5. The thinner air at altitude does not inhibit sprints or so-called anaerobic performances. In fact, sprinters find that there is less air resistance. You may have noticed yourself that it's easier to throw a baseball hard or hit a tennis ball with good velocity at higher altitudes. However, this lack of air resistance does not compensate for the lack of oxygen needed for endurance events.

6. Prior to the 1972 Summer Games in Munich, athletes from many countries were training at altitude for endurance events. Newspapers in Europe at that time made note of the fact in much the same way American papers refer to so-and-so being a good hot-weather baseball player. In other words, the knowledgeable sports fans were led to believe that altitude training was a good thing for those distance runners or rowers.

CPT 10: Doctors, coaches and athletes usually justify training in conditions and altitudes peculiar to their own surroundings.

Since so many countries and their coaches had their athletes training at altitude, apparently they at least believe such training was beneficial.

The Swiss, with their mountainous terrain, have published a lot of in-

45. Uli Wenger, Swiss racer, rests during an altitude training session in the Alps. Local experts in sports medicine believe 2300 meters is optimal for training in high mountains.

formation on altitude training, and they believe in it. On the other hand, the Scandinavians are a bit skeptical about altitude training—but we know their terrain is not like that in the Alps. In the United States you can hear both arguments, depending on where you live or who you talk with.

The controversy here goes like this: The high-country group tells the lowlanders that racing at altitude doesn't make any difference. After the lowlanders catch their breath, they argue the point. The high-country group then says they get logy when they try to perform at sea level. Nonsense, reply the lowlanders. And so it goes.

Training and competing in surroundings natural to you is no doubt a psychological boost and is the major factor for the efficacy of CPT 10.

My own feeling

Here is a wrap-up of mine, based on my experiences at altitude and sea level, and from studies and conversations with some of the world's experts on altitude training. Thus:

1. A lowlander, going to altitude, will find it necessary to slow down his over-all pace of training or racing. Pacing is so important, as always.

2. A lowlander, going to altitude, will probably be at the biggest disadvantage between the fourth and seventh days. Before the fourth day the effects of altitude, on the whole, are not so bad. After the seventh day there is a slow improvement in performance.

3. A highlander, coming to the lowlands to train or race, may feel logy for a few days and an adjustment period is recommended. Eventually he'll have to increase his pace of training or racing in this situation.

4. Training at altitude is unquestionably good if you are going to race at altitude. There's no way around it for the people who live at altitude, so it has to be good.

5. In order for a lowlander to acclimatize fully to altitude, a period of about three weeks is recommended.

Another Altitude Approach

Doctors from Switzerland have gone as far as to determine the optimal altitude for training and they say it's around 2300 m. The theory is that at this altitude the athlete can work hard enough to minimize the danger of deconditioning. (An extreme example might help explain this. Suppose you were situated at very high altitude for a long period of time and that previous to this you had been accustomed to doing a large amount of training at lower levels. You would probably find your capacity to do the same amount of work at high altitude severely hampered, due to the lack of oxygen, so you would do less. After a time you would begin to decondition.) At the same time, at 2300 m, the chemical changes that take place in the body are probably favorable enough to warrant training there. The body produces more red blood cells and hemoglobin at altitude and on coming down to sea level these "extra" RBC will probably increase your oxygen carrying capacity.

The recommended periods of training at altitude are as follows: First an uninterrupted bout of at least three weeks followed by a return for two to four weeks to lower levels for competitions or training. Then, another trip to altitude for about ten days, followed by the final trip to the lowlands for the major competition you have been pointing for. The adjustment period at lower levels will vary with the individual, but a few days should be allowed for this.

Some Disadvantages of Altitude Training

I don't think that altitude training is all peaches and cream. From my own experience watching skiers from this country I have noticed that many skiers who have lived or trained for long periods of time at altitudes have different techniques. These techniques are characterized by slower tempos and more vigorous body movements. I think both traits are natural reactions to altitude. First of all, it's impossible to ski as fast at altitude as at sea level, therefore the slower tempo. The extra body movements like hip wiggles or shoulder twists probably follow for two reasons. If your tempo is slower, especially on a fast track, you have to do something with your body during the gliding phase and even if you have to wait just a fraction of a second, a little extra movement of some sort may help to provide a sort of rhythm. Second, and more arguable, I think the altitude skiers have to "hump" it more in order to get the power they feel necessary for a good stride and thus they put more of their body into each step.

And, since it is difficult to work as intensely at altitude as it is at sea level there is danger of losing some over-all body power at altitude.

In sum: A study of the results of x-c skiers in this country could be interpreted in many different ways. If you are inclined to favor altitude training you could point to any number of cases where it seemed to benefit skiers. Probably the lowlanders who can train occasionally at altitude are in the most favorable situation.

For the future it's likely that opportunity and belief will be the determining factors in our altitude training.

13. Travel & Sickness

If you stay with competition long enough and get proficient, someday you may be making a long trip away from your immediate area in order to race. This is one of the thrills that comes with being a competitor, and every skier I know gets excited about travel.

That long trip

We have learned a few things about extended travel and if you can avoid some of our early mistakes you will be the gainer.

Begin the trip well rested. Some skiers used to take very long workouts just prior to the trip, knowing that they might be a day or two in transit and hence would not be able to ski. That's a mistake. A trip is a workout in itself, and if you go abroad, or go through more than a couple of time zones, your whole daily schedule is going to be thrown off by the time you arrive at your destination.

Change your sleeping schedule before the trip. For instance, if you will be traveling east, before you leave begin going to bed *and* getting up a few hours earlier. This way you will be making some adaptation to the new time schedule at your destination.

Sleep in transit. If you are taking an overnight flight, or if you change several time zones, ask a doctor to prescribe some mild sleeping pills to help you make the transition.

Eat lightly during the flight. Don't eat everything they feed you on most flights: You probably don't need so much and you might as well give your stomach a rest during the first part of your trip. But drink plenty of liquids like juice, tea and water; this will help avoid dehydration.

Regard your flight as a race. After you arrive, regard your trip as a tough race, and figure that every time zone you changed is worth 5 kilometers. For example, in going to Scandinavia from the East Coast we usually go through five time zones. That means that after arriving in Norway, you should behave as if you just finished a 25-km race.

Start training gradually. As an obvious follow-up to travel, you begin skiing slowly in your new surroundings. Don't let your excitement, or the sight of competitors unknown to you, carry you away to the extent of hard workouts too soon. If you wonder how much you should be doing, it's better to do less than more. If you take it easy for a few days you won't suffer. But if you go out and hump it, you may get worn down and increase your chances of catching a cold.

Sickness & Injuries

Getting sick or injured has to be about the most discouraging thing that can happen to an x-c athlete. You train hard for a long period then come to the big event, catch a virus and can't race. In 1972 virtually the whole U.S. Team was sick and could not ski in the Sapporo Olympics at top form. It would take quite a bit of space to recount the details leading up to that experience and I'll just say that what follows is based on talks I've had since then with scores of doctors. Let's look to the future and better luck for all of the competitors.

The best medical coverage

Since a large part of the world's top skiers are receiving the necessary medical attention it's instructive to outline what is being done in some of those instances.

Over-the-Counter

Sometimes during the peak of a racing season athletes feel the need for medication, whether it's a mild sleeping pill, or an antihistamine to knock out some undesirable symptoms. If the athletes' personal physician is at hand, he is the best one to make decisions here. If this advice is not available, beware.

One of my skiers at the 1970 World Championships was nervous the night before a race and, unknown to me, took a sleeping pill on the advice of another athlete who was used to them. However, my skier had never taken a sleeping pill in his life. The result was that he woke up groggy, ate groggy, waxed groggy and raced groggy. His results were groggy too.

Anyone in a high-performance activity should know the effects of any medication he takes. If this knowledge is not available, he should leave the pills alone.

The complete organization has a doctor who is in charge of the athletes. He compiles records of the athletes' medical histories, calls in other specialists as needed (for instance, an orthopedic man might be able to help with one skier's particular problem, or an infectious disease doctor could recommend immunizations), and travels with the team to all important meets. He is the person in the best position to know the skier from a medical point of view. It's quite different for a doctor who is not familiar with the athletes to come along on a trip, armed as he is with all the up-to-date medical information. The new doctor is still missing that important ingredient of familiarity with the athlete.

The team doctor advises the coach on travel and training schedules, diet, vitamin supplements, immunization shots, and prescribes what he feels is necessary. If the doctor is worth his salt, the athletes will gain confidence in him and this team will be better suited to produce optimum results.

The best for the most

As I have said, most of you reading this book will not be lucky enough to have such a situation. So you'll have to listen to Father John's little bits of advice, picked up over the years.

1. If you are sick, for heaven's sake see a doctor. Find out what it is—common cold, flu, virus, etc., and try to determine the recovery period.

2. If you get injured, or pull a muscle, lay off it. See a doctor or a trainer. Get advice.

3. Talk to your doctor about immunization shots. I know all the arguments for and against flu shots. And I look at it this way: Even though I think the shots may not do any good, it's one of those cases where I'll never know. How would I know if the flu shot prevented me from getting the flu? More important, if there is some chance it will do some good, and if I'm real serious about my training program and hoping for good results, it's worth taking the shot as insurance. I know there are people who disagree, but there, I've said it.

4. Aspirin is a wonderful medicine and has all sorts of good qualities. I know one top skier who was on a high dosage of aspirin, prescribed by a doctor for a tendon condition. The aspirin helped the tendon, all right, but the skier started having nosebleeds; and this was very distracting, especially during races. The nosebleeds were caused by the excessive aspirin, because aspirin has anticoagulant properties. Further, the skier developed moderate anemia. "It's not a perfect world," the doctor said. And he's

right. The point is this—if you take a cure of some sort you may have other, and unwanted, consequences. Be prepared.

5. If you travel abroad you should be very careful of your diet. The Norwegians visited France in 1967, a year before the Olympics, and found out what the French vegetables did to their digestive systems; so in 1968 they stayed away from vegetables. Well, you can't whip over to a race site a year early just to taste the food, and so you have to take some ordinary precautions. If you stay away from uncooked food and vegetables, that's a good start. I think you are well advised not to drink water in most of the foreign countries you visit. You can sort of gain a feel for the water and the food, depending on the country you visit. It's an easy thing to boil the water, or have tea or coffee, instead of cold, raw water (and the local tap water may be very raw).

6. Remember that extreme fatigue and cooling lower your resistance to disease, especially colds. You have to avoid this situation. There's no reason for extreme fatigue during the season, except after a long race, and then you should rest up anyway, right after the race.

7. Take care of yourself. I know this sounds simple and obvious, but it isn't that simple for most athletes. Look at it this way: You've trained hard for years and now it's boiling down to a few important races during the winter. Think about what you're doing at this time.

8. Avoid exercises and games that haven't been part of your regular schedule.

9. Avoid crowds as much as possible.

10. Keep on your regular schedule. If it has been producing good results for you don't go off half-cocked on some wild schedule.

11. Saunas are great but there's no firm evidence that taking them will help you sweat out a cold, get rid of that scratchy throat, or otherwise cure you of any infection.

After Sickness

No matter what, you may get sick sometime during the season and then will be faced with the problem of what to do after you get back on skis.

Some gentle training is in order as soon as you feel you're ready to go. If you have three or four days before a scheduled race, take the first couple of days feeling yourself out. Don't overextend, don't get tired. Do some easy distances, then if you feel better, do some short intervals of a few minutes. Sometime before the race you should give yourself a test. In the

case of a senior skier this test doesn't have to be more than 3 to 5 kilometers, but it should be taken, after a warm-up naturally, at racing speeds.
If you feel O.K. during this, you'll probably be O.K. for the race. But, in
the meantime, don't do any more than this.

One of the most difficult situations that arises for a coach is trying to
decide who should race on a given day. To take a tough situation, imagine
having to decide who will run the 4 x 10 men's relay in the Olympic Games.
Two of your best men have been down with colds and are in various stages
of recovery. Do they race? In Japan, during 1972, over half of the coaches
were faced with some problem of sickness on their team. If the athlete is
mature, he will go out and give himself the test I mentioned above, then
tell the coach Yes or No. Norway's most famous relay skier did this in
1972 and told the coach he was not ready. His loss in this race probably

---

For Coaches: Dealing with the Docs

When an athlete is ailing it is your duty to get him to the doctor.
Assess things and set up a recovery schedule right then. There is no
questioning this procedure.

Some doctors, in their eagerness to help the sport, or to study
"healthy bodies," have in the past set up testing situations for the
athletes. These experiments required a moderate amount of the
athletes' time, and unfortunately in a number of cases served only to
provide the doctors with material to write a paper on. (Or, worse, the
papers never got published, so the athletes never learned anything
from the test.)

If you as a coach are approached by the medical profession for
testing of your skiers, sit down with the doctors and study the whole
program. Ask specifically about the follow-up. If there is going to be
a series of tests spread out over a year, or even two, insist on some
consistency of testing so you can measure progress. This can be very
valuable. If there is going to be no feedback to the athletes, you are
better off refusing the tests. This may be tough, since athletes are
usually flattered when asked to serve as guinea pigs, but you should
help them out.

meant the difference between first and second place for Norway. But he was very likely correct in his evaluation of his condition. He had been competing for several years and knew himself well.

If you are just coming off some sort of sickness and have an individual race coming up, you could actually postpone your test until you get in the track, with your number on. If you do this, you must show the maturity to ease up, or even quit the race if you are not feeling well. It does absolutely no good to go out and punish yourself when you are sick. In fact, you might do yourself some further harm.

14. Training Summary

This chapter contains some suggestions for training schedules and you should be very careful in the way you apply them. If you think about the problem of trying to write something for every racer who reads this book you will immediately see many difficulties. Some of you may be juniors, or college students, or persons holding down regular 40-hour-a-week jobs. Some of you may be doing hard physical labor for several hours every day. Imagine my suggesting weight work three times a week for the athletes who are already working at heavy labor all week, or my suggesting 2-300 k's easy skiing a week for a college student approaching exam period.

As usual, you are the one who must learn to judge your best approach to training. What you read here is a compilation of a few norms. You must realize there are exceptions to every schedule. Herewith the most important general Caldwell Principle:

CPT 11: Training is a very individual matter.

After reading this section you should sit down and figure out a program for yourself, using the information you gain here. I've suggested to lots of skiers the following procedure: Calculate the amount of time you have available, especially during the fall and pre-season. Knowing that you will be working at a fairly intense rate just before the heart of the racing season, cast back through the fall and then back through the summer, and plan your program that way—beginning in the spring with fairly easy workouts, in terms of time and intensity, and then slowly increasing during the summer and fall until you work into a schedule you know is realistic for you during the early winter. Make it progressive, in other words.

For sure, every person should have his own schedule planned in advance. It just won't do to look at the day, the weather, or who is doing what, and then decide on the spur of the moment what you are going to do. You must have a well-thought-out plan, and you should follow it. If it doesn't work after a spell, well, of course, make adjustments.

Here goes with a typical schedule I have given to some of the country's top senior skiers, recommending the hours of training to spend per week on cardiovascular workouts. These figures do not include time for strength work, for two reasons. Strength training is very important but it is also the most individual aspect of any program: you should figure out your own best program and go at it (see Chapter 9). Second, as I've hinted above, it doesn't make much sense to include 2 to 4 hours of strength training per week for the fellow who is already doing 40 to 50 hours of manual labor each week.

Cardiovascular Workouts

The following does not include strength workouts (q.v. Chapter 9 and Chapter 10).

Month	Hours per week	Comments
May	8–15	Relaxation, ease into training
June	12–20	Distance and "other"
July	15–20	Distance and "other," roller-skiing
August	15–20	Distance and "other," roller-skiing
September	15–25	Same as August, more roller-skiing
October	15–25	Same as September, introduce intervals
November	15–25	At least half of distance training on snow or roller skis, more interval work
December	15–25	On-snow distance work, technique work, some continuation of intervals and some tempo work (or races)
January	12–25	Same as December, but more tempo work or races; continue intervals
February	12–20	Racing season, easy distance training plus tempo work (or races)
March	12–20	Same as February
April	10–15	Race and relax

As you can see, I have suggested upper and lower limits for each week. Even these are not binding of course. During sickness you would not expect to come up to the lower limit, and during a training camp you would probably exceed the upper limit.

46. Typical amounts of time apportioned to each type of training activity.

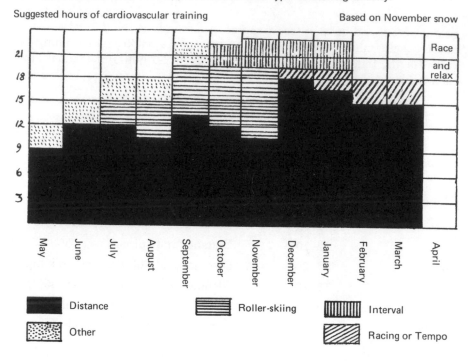

Suggested hours of cardiovascular training

Based on November snow

Distance

Other

Roller-skiing

Interval

Racing or Tempo

47. The curve below has average hours spent in all training over the year. Note increased load in November and December, just before the racing season starts, and the expectable decrease in training sessions during midwinter competition.

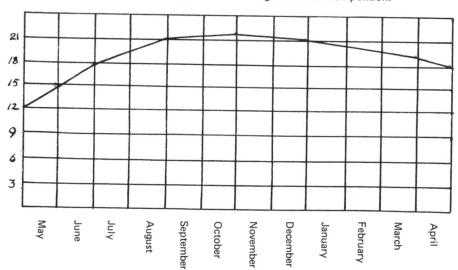

Cardiovascular workouts can also be plotted in the form of a graph, as in Figure 46. If you record your program each week (instead of averaged out per month, as I've done to save space), you will soon be able to check your own trends. Colored penciling works better to differentiate the kinds of workouts than the way they're shown here. You might use blue for distance, black for roller-skiing, red for intervals, yellow for tempo, brown for "other." What you use doesn't matter really, but colors do look nice and may even help give you the gist quicker.

The line graph in Figure 47 is even a faster way to show the seasonal increase and decrease in training load over the year.

Adapting for Junior Skiers

Since the schedules I have outlined above are for senior racers it may be helpful to see another approach to training which involves distance expectations for all ages. The two following tables are adapted from material furnished me by the Finnish Ski Association, for which I am grateful.

Share of Different Training Methods in Training

Total amount of training per year	3000	6000	7500	9000
Running	1300–1400	2000	2500	2500–3000
Roller-skiing	300– 500	500–1000	1000–1500	1500–2000
Skiing	1200–1300	3000 3500	3500–4000	4500

Training Load in Km/year

Age	Males	Females
14	2000	1500–1600
17	3000–4000	2400–3200
20	5000–6000	4000–4800
24	8000–10,000	6400–8000

The increase in training is about 10–20 percent per year.

The amount of training for girls is about 20–25 percent lower than the corresponding amount of training for boys.

48. The Finnish Ski Association upper and lower limits for training volume.

I have taken the Finns' training-load figures beginning with 14-year-olds and put them in the graph (Figure 48) opposite, to illustrate again the general theory of a build-up in training. This time, however, the increase is shown over a period of years instead of during a single season, as in Figures 46 and 47. And it goes to underline my comments at the end of Chapter 1 about the way in which x-c makes such good use of maturity, unlike sports where athletes peak in their 'teens.

Applying Equivalents for Correction

Now turn back to the actual training-load figures on which the graph is based, and it's fairly easy to figure out your average distance per workout. Suppose that you are a 16-year-old female in good shape. You would be expected to log almost 2400 km per year, or around 200 km a month, or about 7 km each day.

There's just one hitch, though. We are not going to let you off easy by allowing you to bike 7 km a day under this schedule.

So here in Putney we have adopted the following procedures for crediting the km's in a workout:

Equivalency Table

	Actual km	Training Log km
Skiing	1	1
Roller-skiing	1	1
Running	1	1
Hiking	1	1
Biking	1	.42
Rowing	1	1.5

Note that these are average comparisons which should be adjusted in the case of biking on flat terrain (where it's easier), rowing a racing shell (which is faster than our ocean shells), etc.

How Much Time?

We can run into apparent complications here. Many of you reading this are students and the natural question is: How can I follow this progressive program idea, the one suggested by the average graph, when I have much more time available in the summer than I do during the fall and the winter?

Well, to answer, it's not so bad.

First let me say that a lot of exercise (training) is good for young people and extra hours spent during the summer, as long as it is enjoyable, will pay off. The Finns say, "Champions are born in the summer."

Next, if you're in this sort of situation with time limitations in the fall and winter, pay very close attention to the intensity of your workouts. Be sure they increase in intensity. In fact, you could substitute a pulse rate scale for the hours-per-week on the vertical axis of the average graph, and then follow that. In other words, increase your average pulse rate instead of the hours-per-week. But since pulse rates vary so much I hesitate to do that for you. However, I have suggested some pulse rates in Chapter 3, and there is the following table.

Type of Workout	Beats per Minute Below Maximum
Distance	40–60
Interval	20–40
Speed	Not taken
Tempo	To be determined by athlete

A few comments about using your table:

First, pulse rate is an individual matter and even the general guidelines given above may not be appropriate for everyone.

Second, in all workouts you should not consciously try to go under. In fact, you should try to avoid it at all times unless you are experimenting, trying to learn the feelings associated with the onset of going under. If you experiment during training you will soon learn your capacities. But, aside from the experiments, don't go under. If this means running a distance workout at more than 60 beats below your max, so be it.

Third, you should expect to be able to work at higher pulse rates as your conditioning improves. For instance, in the early summer your comfortable distance pulse rate might be 60 below max, but in the fall it might be comfortable at only 40–45 below maximum. (This will of course mean that you are going faster, as you would expect.)

Fourth, there is no point in taking your pulse rate during a speed workout. In this kind of exercise you are supposed to go just as fast as you possibly can—usually for a short time period—and knowing your pulse rate is not important.

Finally, when you learn to run your tempo workouts at optimum pulse, you have it! That's pacing.

Little Kids' Training

The world-wide accepted approach to youngsters' development in x-c skiing is this: Let them frolic around and learn to ski until they reach their early 'teens, and then begin a program of more formalized training.

That's fine, but consider this. We usually allow kids aged 1 to 6 to run at random, all day long. The more active ones actually get in good shape—if you don't believe it, try keeping up with a 5-year-old for a day. No way! Then, all of a sudden, when school begins, we put them on buses for daily rides and expect them to sit around in school for 4 to 7 hours a day, five days a week. At this point we have introduced a program of de-training for the kids; they slowly lose their conditioning over the next several years, or until we begin a special program for them.

It doesn't have to be this way. I'm not against education, Lord knows, but it's clear to me that if we allowed more time in school for exercise, or vigorous activity, from age 6 on, it would be more natural and beneficial for the kids. This failing, the parents ought to step in and encourage the little kids to continue their exercise output, or at least give them a freer rein to exercise. They can take it a lot better than most of us realize.

Then, when the kids do reach their 'teens they will be better conditioned to exercise, and training programs will not come as such a shocker.

What Is "Other"?

In the first long table of cardiovascular workouts you will notice an allotment of 2 to 4 hours a week for "other" during the summer months and up until roller-skiing begins to take on a significant time block. For some, "other" could be playing tennis or some skill games. I know that many athletes have their own favorite workout especially suited for the summer months, and they include that. Still others concentrate on an area of their weakness, such as hill climbs, and this would be included under "other."

49. Example of "other." And the girl at right wing always holds her own.

How about Junior Racers?

I have already hinted that juniors do well to take a lot of work, providing it's enjoyable for them. So it's possible some juniors could easily spend as much time as I have suggested for the seniors here. Of course I would not expect them to exercise with the intensity the seniors do.

How Intense?

This is a very individual matter. I have repeatedly said that the intensity should increase, however slowly, during the training season. The pulse rate chart gives some hints. You can take a test run occasionally—remember those? Your times should gradually improve for the test runs (it could be a hike, a bike, a row, some intervals, or whatever) and this is usually indication enough that your intensity of training has increased.

And remember the rule-of-thumb that you should not get really stiff during a workout. If you do, you're probably going too hard.

How about Distance *vs* Intervals *vs* Tempo, Etc.?

I think distance training, as I've rather loosely defined it, should take 60–80 percent of your training time. The bar graph (Fig. 46) bears this out. Keep in mind that distance training should be done on x-c terrain and that it necessarily will include periods of greater stress, followed by recovery periods. During the fall and early season you should increase the formal amount of interval training and this is indicated on the graph. But there are no clearly defined percentages to go by, mainly because of the close connection between good distance training for x-c and good interval training.

You should introduce roller-skiing about 3 to 4 months before on-snow skiing. Normally this will be counted for distance training unless you have some very special terrain and transportation features which allow you to do strict interval training. I would not suggest this, at any rate. As you begin roller-skiing you will ease off in your other distance training, but don't give it up completely. Roller-skiing three to four times a week just before the snow flies is adequate.

You noticed that tempo training had crept in on the bar graph earlier. Recall that this is training at racing speed. I would include also, therefore, time spent in races as tempo training.

What about Weather?

The weather, especially in New England, is an important factor in any program. I like to think we have it licked here in Putney. Aside from the problem of over-all snow conditions, which are probably not as good as those in some other parts of the country, there are the vagaries of daily weather to contend with throughout the year. No matter where you are, it's a temptation to postpone or cancel a workout because of inclement weather. This is bad.

There are a few situations which would preclude an out-of-doors workout but I can't think of many. (If the weather is very cold and windy the risk of exposure could be dangerous, for instance.) However, athletes and coaches too often change their plans because of weather.

"It's raining and I don't like to run in the rain."

"It's too hot."

"It's too cold, too slippery, too something."

Bah-h! Who's in charge here, anyway? You or the weather?

I observed some U.S. Combined jumpers waiting-out "bad conditions" for a week preceding a World Championship event. First, the inrun was

50. But sometimes it's even more fun in the rain . . .

too slick and the boys did not jump. Next, it was too windy. Then a day came along when the conditions were perfect and everyone trained. However, the next day produced slick inrun tracks again. "No jumping for us." Everyone else was jumping, however. The competition day came and the conditions were identical with those of the "bad days." Naturally, our team did not fare so well.

A good rule-of-thumb is to proceed with your scheduled workout unless it poses a high risk of injury or harm to the body. If you cater to the weather you'll never learn to be a mudder. On the other hand, if you train regardless of weather you'll feel better for it—and will also gain an advantage on the fellows who are fair-weather athletes.

"Neither snow, nor rain, not heat, nor gloom of night stays these athletes from the swift completion of their appointed workouts."

Alone, or in Groups?

There's no doubt that training in groups is beneficial to most athletes. And there are advantages to training alone too. The intelligent athlete will do both.

In a group there is usually some added incentive or competition which makes people train harder. Group trips or runs, bikes, hikes, etc., are often more fun than solos.

In most training situations in our area there is a very strong feeling of togetherness and not a great deal of emphasis on individual performance. There is a long-range benefit to this approach. Friendships are furthered, and even long-remembered traditions are established.

This attitude separates x-c from many other sports where some people are very secretive about their methods of training, or even about their equipment. And when people do train in situations like these they often do so mainly to check up on their competition.

But there are two obvious dangers to relying solely on group training. First, if you depend on a group, or even on someone else to go training with, there will come a day when you won't go out, or you will be delayed because the other party isn't there or isn't ready. Second, if you train in a group all the time you will find that the range in abilities tends to telescope in. The weaker athletes get pulled along faster and this is good for them. But the stronger athletes lack the incentive to go harder because they are already riding on top, and so they often don't develop as much as they might otherwise. (To be on top and to stay on top is tough. It requires extra effort and push all the time. You can't stop too often to look over your shoulder, either.)

There are two clear advantages to training alone. First, you can go out whenever you want to. You don't have to depend on anyone else. Second: as they say, when you're racing you're usually alone out there, so you better find out what it's like.

If you can train alone and increase your workload, push yourself harder, and all that, the chances are better that you will be more successful than you would be after most often training in a group.

In sum: Aside from the atmosphere or location of your x-c training, it is clear that the following principles hold:

The tougher the competition you are going to enter, the longer you have

51. "Flawless" is the word for Oddvar Braa, showing his World Cup winner's form as he cruises by the great Putney Elm.

to train. Five to eight years is probably the minimum required to reach a level of international competence.

Your training should be varied and enjoyable. Boy, it can be hard work, and you better be able to enjoy it!

Specificity training is very important. This means not just technique training on snow, but includes a lot of special drills in your dry-land program.

Your program must be progressive.

Crash programs are too risky. Your program must have regularity: It's better to get your kilometers in during a longer period of time than to telescope the k's into a shorter period of time.

A Note for the "Citracer"

Now is a good time to issue the standard warnings to the casual citizen racer, the one who does not have a regular training program, yet decides to "go for it" at some regional race during the winter that draws upward of a thousand entrants.

In general, don't extend yourself. Make finishing the tour your primary goal. There is no point in straining when you are not in condition. You will just be fooling yourself and may court an injury or feel so poorly after the race that you will be discouraged from further events.

Don't think that a crash program of training will prepare you to compete with skiers in your age class who have been training regularly for months, or even years. Let them ski their race; if you are unhappy about your results, make up your mind to be in better shape for next year's event.

Don't pick out the longest, toughest race in your area for your one appearance of the year. Be reasonable: Enter some race that is within your limits.

Most citraces have classes by age groupings and gender. Be content to compete with the skiers in your class. If there are a few ringers in your class—members or alumni of the U.S. Ski Team, for instance—be grateful for the opportunity to ski *with* them. Don't worry about skiing *against* them.

Honing Co-ordination

Co-ordination exercises and sports are very good training for improving your technique. I'm not talking now about specificity exercises or actual on-snow skiing, but other types of exercise which require a high degree of co-ordination. Tumbling, diving, modern dance, team sports, tennis—these are just a few. Good coaching in these will increase their value to your skiing. The advantages of these types of exercise are evident.

They are diversionary, often a good break from the rugged routine of training.

By getting coaching in movements not necessarily specific to your sport you nevertheless improve your ability to respond to directions or coaching, and this will probably aid your technique. I've seen lots of skiers improve their technique over the summer without doing any ski-related exercises. (I think your own thinking processes can be improved by co-ordination training of this sort.)

Finally, certain elements in these co-ordination exercises are good for anyone. Some increase your flexibility, your reaction, your strength and your enjoyment of sports.

---

15. Skiing *Well*

Skiing well, using the very finest points of technique, is a very subtle thing. The best x-c skiers in the world adapt to different conditions instinctively and cannot necessarily tell you what they are doing, or why they are doing it. Still others actually can think about all the ramifications of a given situation and proceed to apply their skill in the most effective manner.

In countries with a long tradition of x-c, many skiers and coaches talk about the niceties of technique with the same ease as American students of baseball do about their national pastime. At the World Junior Championships in 1979, in Quebec, I heard one Finnish coach explaining to his skiers that "today it is very important to pay attention to maintaining momentum during the frequent shifts from double-poling to single stride, and back again." Some other coaches apparently thought it was enough simply to urge their skiers to go fast. It all reminded me of rookie baseball coaches telling their batters to hit the ball well, while the more seasoned coach might tell his hitters to watch carefully the way the infielders were leaning with each pitch.

In North America we are relatively new to the sport of x-c skiing and we must study and analyze the different techniques necessary for different conditions in an effort to close the gap on the more experienced skiers and coaches from abroad.

In sum: Generally the value of technique is tremendously underestimated even by racers in North America, many of whom train as hard as anyone in the world, but with results that fall short because they can't ski. Well, of course they can ski; I mean that they can't ski with finesse—which means with skill. Some of these racers need less time pounding the pavements and more time spent on roller skis, or co-ordination exercises, or concentrated on-snow sessions to hone their technique.

Yet some racers and coaches remain bullheaded and cite as examples the Norwegians, who rarely practice technique. (Remember CPT 1—the disarray in approaches to training?) And it's true, the top Norwegians rarely do practice their technique. It should be understood, however, that Norway has so many good skiers and the competition for her teams is so fierce, that if anyone does make the team it can be assumed he has good technique. Or else he wouldn't make it to the top.

For years the situation in the United States favored some of the older skiers who had been on deck a long time, who skied fairly well—and,

52. Classic x-c technique from both sides of the Atlantic. Oddvar Braa (left) and Magne Myrmo (right), from Norway, bracket Tim Caldwell of the U.S. Team.

most important, were the strongest guys on the scene, the fellows in the best shape. Now, though, there are more racers around, so technique is becoming an increasingly important factor. It's no longer possible to train your way onto many of the teams in this country.

I feel confident that eventually our technique in the United States will improve. That's one of the reasons for writing this book. So here's the first Caldwell Principle of Technique (CPTK):

CPTK 1: All the best kinds of training will not be a guarantee of good race results: you must know how to ski well.

And It's a Wonderful Feeling

Anyone who has ever skied rapidly over the terrain with seemingly fluid motion knows what it feels like to be at one with the trail and the surroundings. There is a certain flowingness, almost as if the ups and downs in the track are unrolling under you, and you're just waiting for more to come along. The effort required to ski fast with good rhythm adds to the rewards of that feeling.

I've done all the types of skiing events there are, and each has its special flavor, but x-c is just something else! It's the most natural and the most diversified, full of new experiences, and the healthiest. There are more thrills than you can count. And the feeling of accomplishment after an outing is unmatched, whether it's been a cruise through the woods with my family, or a 30-km tour with visiting members of the national team from Australia.

Waxing

Waxing deserves some comment now because it plays such a large part in determining your technique. For instance, if your skis are slippery you will find a shuffling technique may be best. At the other end of the scale, if your skis are iced, you will have to run or bound along. (We always strive for a good wax job so we can try to ski properly, but . . .)

In a cross-country ski race waxing is probably the most important factor that does not lend itself to nearly complete control or preparation. No matter what you do for training, no matter how good your technique, no matter how good your coaching and equipment, you can always get out-waxed sometime and come in with results below your potential.

No doubt there is enough material to write a book on waxing, but such is not my intent here. Why not? Well, I've always been leery of really expanding on waxing for the following reasons.

First, waxing is continually changing. Wax brands change. Wax companies bring out new waxes yearly. Skis and their bases change. Obviously it's rather difficult to keep information on waxing updated, because the production of a book takes so long.

Second, waxing is more of an art than any other aspect of x-c and is best learned by a lot of practice. I can tell you to smooth the wax and how to do it, but that does not mean you can simply read about it and then wax well.

Finally, wax that works well for one person may not work well for another. I recall prescribing wax for my Putney team one spring. We were using klister and I had fourteen skiers to contend with. I squeezed the stuff on their skis, putting it just where they told me to, and they smoothed it out. Eight skiers liked the wax, three said it was too slick and three said it was too grabby and slow. The main point here is that the reaction to the same wax varied so widely.

So, no waxing book yet. You are the one who will be using your skis and you should determine how to wax them under all conditions. Even my beginning Putney School skiers are expected to learn waxing by the end of their first season.

However, here are a few tips.

Always wax for the uphills. Several studies have shown what many of us always suspected: Uphills are the place where you spend the most time, and where you also can gain or lose the most time. If you have slippery skis you stand to lose a lot of time and energy. So beware.

Testing klister. In testing for climb in klister conditions (generally granular snow) it usually works to test your skis on the flats. If they work here they surely will climb since you will be using a more vigorous kick (see below) there.

Testing for powder. In hard-wax conditions (powder) I test my skis on an average uphill to see if I can make it up the grade without using my poles. If I can, the wax is about right for racing. I'll have the added advantage of using my arms and poles in a race, but I may lose some purchase, or hold, because of the wax wearing off, or because I am not able to ski properly, or because I am tired.

The kicker. A controversy has been brewing in the United States over the advantages of the long kicker *vs.* the short kicker. But long or short is not really the question. The point is to have skis that hold well for you while you're climbing hills. If you can climb efficiently with a short kicker, and ski the flats as well, that is good. If you need a longer kicker for the hills, put it on.

Ski stiffness. The ease with which you climb, or ski the flats using good technique, depends on several factors. These include your strength and technique, the slope of the hill you are on, the wax (naturally), *and* the degree of your skis' stiffness.

Most skiers have two different stiffnesses in skis. The stiffer one is used primarily in klister conditions, the softer one mainly in powder. Naturally there are "soft" klister skis and "stiff" powder skis, and sometimes racers use powder skis for klister conditions (when the going is soft) and klister skis for powder conditions (when the track is very hard). But as a rule it's klister skis for klister snow and powder skis for powder snow.

I favor using a ski—whether it's a powder or a klister ski—that is soft enough to be flattened against the snow without my having to jump on it, or press down hard. With such a ski—which some will claim is slower on downhills because of its softness—I can actually feel the track and the wax coming in contact with it, and therefore have better control over the effort in my kicking motion. In addition, I can usually wax harder, or use a faster wax under the foot, than someone with stiffer skis. As a result my skis might be as fast as, or faster than, the stiffer ones.

In general, stiffer skis will require softer wax for climbing, while softer skis will not require wax so soft.

Now perhaps you can understand why the six dissatisfied skiers cited above did not find my wax prescription satisfactory. Their skis were probably a mixture of powder and klister models, or were stiffer or softer for them than the average flex of the eight others' skis.

In sum: There's no doubt that waxing gets complicated. But, to reiterate, you are the best one to figure out your own wax. Meanwhile don't get psyched by what another competitor is using for wax. He may have different needs. If your wax works well, go with it.

How waxing affects technique

A certain amount of simplification and generalizing is needed here. Suffice it to say that I believe the information that follows will apply in over 90 percent of the waxing situations you will encounter.

Generally, we have klister conditions or powder-snow conditions, and generally the wax works or it doesn't work. Thus there are four cases to consider.

Case No. 1: Good Klister Wax

Klister conditions usually permit a more vigorous kicking motion, especially on the uphills. Therefore the uphill techniques can entail longer strides and possibly more motions like bounding. The body position may be farther forward than for powder snow. Shuffling is not so effective.

On the flats the forward glide is accomplished mainly as a result of a vigorous kick with the rear leg and a relatively passive forward leg movement, or thrust. There is a nearly imperceptible delay—as compared to powder-snow skiing—in shifting the weight onto the gliding ski.

Case No. 2: Good Powder Wax

Powder snow, even though it is hard packed, is best suited for a less hard, more drawn-out (to the extent of a few thousandths of a second) kick, as compared to the klister-wax kick. Shuffling is easy and effective, especially on uphills, in powder snow. There can be more reaching ahead with the forward leg, and the actual effort put forth by both legs in powder snow is more nearly equal—though still not truly equal since the kicking leg supplies most of the power.

Cases 3 & 4: Bad Wax, Powder or Klister

My comments so far give some guidance for skiing with wax that is less than ideal. Short of icing up, there are two extremes we encounter: the skis can be too slow, or they can be too slippery.

Slow skis. Generally, skis that are too slow have fairly good grip and you must make the most of this situation by skiing hard uphill, even running if possible. You will have to take the downhill sections as they come and not be bothered by the fact that here your skis are rather slow. On downhills, extra work for speed will not pay off as much as extra effort does on the uphills.

On the flats you must try to ski at slightly slower than top speed, by using a high tempo without a lot of power in each kick. You will just run yourself under if you work too hard to push your skis when they are slow.

Fast skis. Slippery skis are generally fast (but would you believe that some skis that don't hold are slow as well?), and you should accommodate in the following ways to take advantage of them:

On downhills, crouch and go for long runouts; or use a lot of double-poles if you are not going too fast to do so.

On flats you will have to use double-poling almost exclusively.

On uphills you may have to give away a bit of time by using more herringbones than another fellow does. But this is the place you will have to work hardest, just the same.

With a choice between a slippery or slow ski, most skiers would prefer having a slick one, so long as they can herringbone with good effect and have a very strong double-pole. Those who are not in good shape will probably be better off with a slower ski that climbs better.

For Coaches: Setting Up Tests

It's always interesting to form a theory, or wonder about some aspect of technique in x-c, and then design an experiment involving several skiers to test it out.

Basically, all you have to do to test something is set up an experiment and eliminate all but one of the variables. Run your test, study the results, and come out with your conclusion. It's perfectly easy, I tell my coaching friends (with tongue in cheek).

Here's an example. I wanted to test two uphill roller-skiing techniques, so I got five or six skiers to repeat the hill runs several times, alternating techniques, and recording their pulse rates at the top of the hill. I stood by and took their times for each run. I thought that if we came up with one technique that took less time and also produced a lower heart rate at the top of the hill, we would really have something.

However, during the test I could see it would not be valid because the skiers were not proficient enough in using the two different techniques. Maybe next season.

We weren't discouraged, though. It was a workout, it was interesting. And the skiers did get a good chance to practice techniques.

Here's one *you* can try on snow.

Pick out a good, long stretch of double-poling terrain, and have one set of skiers use the no-step technique and another group use the one-step, and take times and pulse rates. Next, have the skiers switch to the other technique, and check the results. Then compare the times and pulse rates for the no-step with those for the one-step, to see if you can reach any conclusion.

Glazed Track Conditions

Glazed tracks often present many wax problems and racers may end up with skis that are too slick, or too slow. You should use your skis according to the advice given above.

I think we will find more and more instances of waxless skis being used by racers in these conditions, and if you are really eager, you will have to keep abreast of new developments.

It should be clear that it's a good idea to practice occasionally with far from perfect skis. A tendency in training, since there is not so much time pressure, is to wax and rewax as you go along, until your skis are just right for every condition you meet. Maybe next time you'd better keep skiing with what you started with. You will soon find out if you can run the hills, or use a good herringbone. And I can't tell you how much my arms have been developed using the good ol' "take-me-home" double-pole.

16. Technique for the Flat

There has been more discussion, and more material published, on flat technique than on all the other x-c techniques combined. This is natural, for a couple of reasons.

First, it's easy, and usually pleasant, to stand around on the flats and watch skiers, comparing methods against results. Here you can see skiers for long stretches and study the repetition of their movements. It's different on downhills, where the skiers whisk by so suddenly that viewing them is more difficult; then, by the time they stop far below, communication is hampered. On uphills the problem is one of time, not distance: Skiers can't run uphills for so long as they can on the flats or the downhills, so time for evaluation is severely limited.

Next, uphills require so many different techniques—each dictated by the snow conditions, your wax, your skis, and the pitch of the hill—that it's difficult to get a situation where you can single out one or two facets of technique to concentrate on.

Finally, the most common image we have of accomplished x-c skiers is like the one offered in Photo 52, where they are stretched out and cruising, just motoring along in full elegance. So why shouldn't we talk a lot about flat skiing? That's where I will begin.

Where the power is

Any knowledgeable racer will tell you that the main power for the single stride is derived from the kick of the leg, downward and back. This is obvious. And the trouble is that it's *too* obvious and many skiers and coaches stop thinking right here. They don't consider the extra benefit that can be gained from the pendulum-like, forward swing of the nonkicking leg and of the arm.

To consider the kick alone as the propelling force is a bit like thinking in terms of a cyclist pushing only down on the pedals and ignoring the pulling up. Or, it's the same kind of thinking that leads one to believe that in operating one end of a two-man crosscut saw you should only pull and not push a little as well (at the right time of course).

Several years ago I began to approach the single stride by putting emphasis on what I called forward leg-drive. I'm convinced this approach has worked well and now I have one method of teaching skiing which emphasizes forward leg-drive alone.

Forward Leg-drive *and* Kick

The best skiers in the world do kick down and back—*and* they also drive their opposite leg ahead, simultaneously and with great power.

The not-so-good skier relies on kick alone; and he's the one in trouble when his wax slips, or the track disintegrates beneath him. Generally the kick-type skier, as I'll call him, is good on klister snow, or on granular conditions where he can kick like a mule and go like the wind. But get him out on some loose stuff or a soft track and he often looks like a beginner. This is because he does not sneak up on his kick gently: instead, he almost pounds his rear ski into the track. So it is with skiing; and you can't always come down hard on the track, and you shouldn't.

There is an added inefficiency in being a kick-skier. Lots of times the extra kick does little more than break down the snow in the track, thus wasting some power. In a race, this costs you.

One good method for testing how much you depend on your kick is to ski with slippery wax, or with no wax at all. Then if you kick too hard, you just slip and don't really go anywhere. I've experimented with teach-

53. Storybook conditions for a skier Down Under: the big sky, bright sun, about 3° Celsius, and gum trees along the route. This Australian routinely waxes for such glazed conditions, which most North Americans prefer to stay away from.

ing people about more forward leg-drive by having them use slippery skis, and the example often helps.

It might be easy to get the impression that I am endorsing a pussyfoot sort of technique. Not so. See if you can determine for yourself the differences between the top skiers, the ones who kick hard only and don't have any forward leg-drive, and the ones who have forward leg- or knee-drive in addition to a good kick. It all happens so fast that advocates of either system by itself, as being the sole method to use, might be convinced by watching a good skier that he is using the method they opt for. But chances are he's using both the forward drive and the kick.

I'm going to talk about three or four important components of good technique for skiing on the flat. In addition to the forward leg-drive and the kick, there are other aspects such as the arm-swing and momentum.

Forward leg-drive

In each stride the rear leg begins to swing forward with a relatively slow, pendulum-like motion. This slow movement doesn't last very long, though, and it accelerates. I often describe this forward swing of the leg as being similar to the arm motion used by a fast-pitch softballer. Some pitchers pause briefly, with their pitching arm high over their heads, then the arm swoops down, accelerating, and swings forward with a very fast motion just before the ball is released. So it is with the rear leg in skiing: it swings down, accelerating all the time, and then drives forward.

Common mistakes in the leg-swing are to accelerate too fast and then stop the forward drive too soon; or to have no forward drive at all; or not to accelerate but rather just to swing the foot and leg through in a lackadaisical manner.

The "Level-feet" Problem

Some coaches place occasional emphasis on where the foot should be when the ski hits the snow on its forward swing. They will say the feet should be exactly opposite before the ski really hits the snow— an injunction that sometimes leads skiers to lift their forward leg slightly as it swings through. This lifting is a mistake and will detract from your power. I've seen all sorts of top skiers whose forward-swinging foot hits well before the opposite, more stationary, foot. They don't have any secrets. It's just that their foot is coming through so fast

54 (near strip) **& 55** (frames far right). You might call these vertical sequences an international blueprint for the diagonal as you compare the skier at left with the one on the right. Although from different countries, these top racers show few, if any, differences in form.

146

that it doesn't matter where it hits. It's also coming *forward*, and as long as the motion is forward, and fast, it hardly matters where the foot hits. Maybe it is a couple of cm's behind the other. So don't worry too much about where that foot should hit.

As the feet pass, you should continue to exert pressure on your forward-swinging leg, from the foot and on up. Your knee gets into the act, then the upper leg just above the knee; and then, with some skiers, the hips contribute to the thrust.

The Hip Problem

Warning: Some skiers use a lot of hip motion, which is acceptable under certain conditions—if your tempo is low, for example. If perforce you are skiing slowly you can take time to twist the hips a bit, but with fast tempo there is hardly time to twist the hip forward, then untwist it.

A worse situation occurs when a skier initiates his forward leg-drive with the hip. By doing this he loses the opportunity to get that slingshot effect of swinging through with the leg, beginning with the foot, at maximum speed.

These hippers look powerful sometimes, but don't worry about them. They almost never score.

Finally, you can look at it this way. X-C racing is getting yourself around the track in the fastest man-

ner. During the single stride this is accomplished by first powering one ski ahead down the track, then the other, and so on. Clearly, the fellow who gets his ski ahead the fastest is going to have an advantage. Suppose his every forward leg-swing takes just a fraction of a second less than his competitors'—well, there are a lot of strides in a race and these fractions add up.

So, as long as your forward leg-drive accelerates, at least until your legs pass one another, it can never come through too fast. Remember that. Of course momentum and glide are other considerations and these will be covered below.

The kick

There's no doubt that the kicking leg in each stride needs to have its ski somewhat anchored to the snow or track. This anchoring is done by setting the wax, which in turn usually is accomplished by a downward push through the ski onto the snow. This motion is often accompanied by a little hitch in the leg— really a slight flexing of the knee just before the final and more vigorous push down-and-back.

The key to the kicking phase of the stride is to get as much thrust along the track as possible, without slipping. Imagine how much kick, and therefore thrust along the track, you could get by pushing straight back. It would be similar to the thrust a swimmer gets when he turns and kicks off the wall at one end of the pool. Of course your kick is never this effective, but it's something to think about.

Snow conditions and the wax you are using have a lot to do with the kind of kick you utilize. As I've hinted, in klister-snow conditions only poor wax will prevent you from having all the kick you need: you can horse it here, kicking hard and even later than normal, and using maximum power. On packed powder, on the other hand, you may find it necessary to kick down into the track a bit sooner, or to kick less vehemently. If you think about it, you'll find concentrating on the forward leg-drive will help here too.

If the kick is powerful the leg will straighten out behind. To many observers it will look as if the rear leg does not really straighten out and this leads some coaches to tell their skiers they aren't kicking hard enough, etc. However, with the expert skiers it takes good photography actually to show the leg straightening out, it all happens so fast. The leg whips back and, like a rubber band, immediately recoils slightly. This immediate recoil is relaxing and a part of good technique.

If the kick is not powerful, the leg of course will not straighten out behind, and the skier will not go too fast. Beginner skiers have this fault occasionally, and it's usually

because they have not developed the balance or the strength necessary to ski properly, with good power.

So now we have two things to think about. While one leg starts swinging forward in a relaxed manner the other leg is tensed and making a real power stroke—the kick. Then, the roles are reversed and the kicking leg relaxes while the forward-swinging leg takes over and drives ahead. It sounds easy and it is, if you don't try and analyze it so much that it slows down your movements. Remember, these actions take place with lightning speed.

The arm-swing

I've seen lots of skiers get their stride mixed up by trying to do something special with their arms. For sure, if you can move your arms and legs naturally, as you do in walking, you won't have to worry much about co-ordinating the movements of all your limbs. But there are several elements of the arm-swing that seem so important to me that I want to discuss them here. I have had good success in approaching most technique problems by concentrating on slight changes in arm movements. So I will break the arm-swing down into two components, mainly for the sake of analysis. Don't get the idea that because I talk about the power stroke (or backswing) and the forward arm-swing, these movements actually are separated in a herky-jerky manner. If you think about using the arms as you use your legs—that is, using both the forward leg-drive and the kicking motion down and back to propel yourself along the track— you will be on your way to attaining proper technique.

In general, use your arms like the conductor of an orchestra, to help direct the motions of the rest of the body. Hold on, though!—whatever you do, don't wave your arms like a maestro; instead, use them to control your leg tempo and your body position.

And don't force anything with the arms. For instance, don't force your arm straight ahead and hold it there just because someone tells you to. Or don't swing the arm across in front of your body just because you see someone else doing it.

The Power Push

I'll define the power push as that part of the poling motion which occurs from the instant the pole basket hits the snow until the arm begins its forward swing again. Or look at it this way: as soon as the basket hits the snow you should begin to get a push from it. This push is initiated by a tensing of the hand, wrist and forearm and a downward motion of the forearm. Two of the most common errors in poling are

(1) planting the pole too far ahead and having to ski by it before any downward pressure can be applied, and (2) pulling the forearm back slightly, parallel to the track, before beginning the downward push or thrust. Neither of these bad habits will do.

As the strong, downward motion of the forearm continues, the rest of the poling arm and shoulder assists so greatly that, with a strong skier, the arm is almost flung to the rear.

This power stroke should continue to be vigorous until the arm passes the hip. It's fairly easy to check this by standing to the side of a skier and looking for daylight between the poling arm and the hip.

With a Flick of the Wrist

One new gimmick being used by several U.S. racers is flicking the wrist before the arm's power push is completed, or just as the hand gets to the hip. The wrist flicks, the hand opens momentarily to let go of the pole, then the hand grasps the pole handle again for the forward arm-swing. These wrist-flickers end up with their wrist cocked at almost a right angle to their forearm. It's a means for relaxing the arm, I suppose.

This premature relaxing of the arm usually causes a related, more serious, flaw in technique: Often the flick triggers a relaxation of the whole body, and everything stops, particularly the forward leg-drive. For a moment such skiers look like statues. All I can say is that it's a very relaxing way to ski, but not a very fast way to race, because any skier will slow up and lose momentum if the forward leg-drive stops too soon.

Still, if the wrist-flick does not in any way inhibit the forward leg- or knee-drive, then I would admit, begrudgingly, that there isn't much power lost in the stride—only that small amount that can be gained by using the arms properly.

In sum: For good (meaning efficient) technique, the wrist and hand should act as extensions of the forearm— the wrist is kept stiff, and in line with the forearm—until after the arm passes the body on its power push to the rear. Then, the hand opens, the fingers point down toward the track or toward the tail of the ski, the arm relaxes momentarily, and the hand grasps the pole again for the forward swing.

The Forward Arm-swing

I've been talking about the backswing of the arm being the power push, and that's true. This is a strength you can develop in your dry-land training. But the forward arm-swing is really a more subtle motion, and the differences evident in the use of this forward swing separate the good skiers from the also-rans.

In addition to dictating tempo, the forward swing of the arm should be used to keep your body in a proper position and to maintain momentum in your stride. The arm should swing forward in concert with the rest of the body in a way to help you get down the track as fast and as smoothly as possible.

Consider an arm-swing that is rather stiff, fast, and perhaps too early. The effect of it would be to set your butt back slightly, as if you were about to sit down. Alternatively, if the arm-swing is too late and your upper body is already well forward, the swing will be incomplete and will not help to generate maximum forward momentum—unless of course you really extend your arm, in which case you take a chance on tipping over forward.

In sum: There is no one speed and method for swinging the arm forward. It all depends on the condition of the track. For instance, on a very fast track, which allows a little more time in each stride because the glide is longer, the good skier will delay his arm-swing ever so slightly at the beginning—not by holding his arm in an extended position behind him, but by starting the forward motion more slowly than usual. Or, sometimes a skier will swing an arm forward at about the usual rate but actually cross it slightly in front of his body, just to take a little more time. (Hence my earlier warning about not mimicking others' idiosyncrasies: If a good skier crosses his arm in front he may do it only under these conditions.)

Actually, fast tracks that require a change in arm tempo are pleasant problems to be faced with, and you can learn a lot about your own ski-ing under these conditions. You may find your timing is off, or that you are working too hard for the speed you generate.

Momentum

The true technician will ski in such a way as to maintain his momentum no matter what comes along, espe-

---

That Clipped Arm-swing

One of the most recent faults to show on the scene is the short, or clipped, front arm-swing, where the arm comes forward with a severely bent elbow and the hand comes up right in front of the face. By doing this a skier loses all chance of gaining momentum from his forward arm-swing and therefore loses some glide and efficiency.

This short arm-swing has probably evolved during the last few years because of the too-stiff skis being used and because of certain bad habits developed in roller-skiing.

With the stiff skis one must put out more effort to set the wax. This stomping-down motion leads naturally to a shortened arm-swing. Try it for yourself.

Further, with certain roller skis the utmost in good balance and concentration is required in order to allow the arm to swing forward in a relaxed, easy, yet powerful manner. The result is that skiers who don't maintain balance and concentration cheat on the length of their arm-swing, and thus on their glide, and thus on their technique.

This problem has become so severe with some skiers that I have splinted their arms and made them practice without being able to bend their arms at all, just so they could get the feeling of a decent arm-swing.

Another way to help correct this deficiency is to ask the skier to be sure his hand is as low as is possible without drooping the shoulder, and that his hand is relaxed as it swings by the hip.

cially on flat terrain; he can do change-ups, go into double-poling, ski around corners, or do anything else without losing his speed. The novice will show a noticeable decrease in speed in doing these things. If you have been watching skiers for a long time it's easy to focus on this aspect. Squint until the skier is just a blob on the landscape—pay no attention to arms, legs, body position, etc. Then ask the blob to go from a diagonal stride to a double-pole, or to ski using the diagonal around a slight corner. Check to see if the blob decelerates.

Deceleration

Deceleration is usually caused by faulty body position. The skier is not forward far enough to be able to ski off the ball of his foot, whether he's going into a double-pole, a change-up, or skiing a corner. One method of keeping forward is to use the arms properly, because if your arms swoop forward at the right time you'll be all set.

Skiing Corners

A wonderful practice for learning to keep your momentum is to ski a large figure-eight on, say, a soccer field. Make the curves flat enough so you must ski, rather than *skate*,

56. Taking a corner at full stride means starting the turn with the outside ski.

the turns. (Occasionally there will be one or two little skate turns in there, but that's O.K.) As you ski around, check your momentum to see if you can ski the left corners as well as the right ones.

There are two basic methods for skiing corners. Let's go around a left turn.

1. You can slide the right ski forward and stem it slightly to the left with each stride, and then bring the left ski alongside.

2. Or, you can pivot the left ski on its shovel when it is in its rearmost position. Just twist it slightly, aiming it more to the left, and scoot it forward with your next leg-drive; in this instance bring the right ski alongside.

The better skiers use a combination of both these methods. However, in general you should initiate your turn with the outside ski. Too many skiers begin with the inside ski.

Checking for Momentum

You may not realize why you are losing momentum at certain times, and the best way to find out is to ski with a friend who is more powerful or better than you are. With his permission, jump in right behind him and follow him so closely that occasionally your ski tip clicks his ski tail.

Matching him stride for stride will give you an opportunity to compare lots of facets of technique. Do you appear to kick as hard?—to drive your leg forward as hard, as fast, and as far? Are your arm motions synchronized with his? Do you have any extra upper-body motions that impair your ability to keep up with him? Do you move as quickly, and do you relax as long—and are you working as hard? Do you keep up with him when going from single-poling to the double-pole, then back to single-poling again?

Try to analyze your technique against his, and then see if you can make adjustments in your efficiency through practice and training.

CPTK 2: The ability to maintain momentum is one of the most valuable aspects of good technique.

Style Differences

There is always a danger in trying to copy someone, or in trying to determine proper technique by analyzing another person's skiing. Body builds vary, strengths vary, even the skis and waxes one uses dictate technique in part. If you pick out one skier you know, one who happens to be a top racer, and compare him with other international stars, chances are you will find several dissimilarities. Don't worry. Assess his ability according to:

CPTK 3: Good technique means having good forward leg-drive; a good kick; using the arms to help

154

57. The U.S.S.R. relay team, winners of the World Junior Championships held at Mont Ste-Anne, Québec, February 1979. From left: Alexandre Koutoukine, Alexandre Tchaiko, Serguei Nichkov.

get along the track and to help main tain momentum. And maintaining momentum, period.

Yet winning form can be canceled by small losses of concentration and resulting failure to apply all the things you've learned:

CPTK 4: In tough competition you must get an A in Academics, which includes Attention.

If any skier has all these attributes, then he has good technique, no matter what quirks he may have in his style (such quirks as bobbing his head slightly or crossing one arm in front of his body, and so on).

The double-pole

First, I'll dispose of the two- or three-step double-poles. These are an old-fashioned technique in which skiers took two or three steps forward preparatory to using both poles simultaneously. Taking this many steps is both unnecessary and slow.

So we're left with the one-step double-pole and the no-step double-pole—both very valuable. There are many similarities between the diagonal technique and these two double-poles. I'll hit on them throughout.

How Skis & Conditions Dictate

It is important to stress the main distinctions between the one-step double-pole and the no-step double-pole. When I wrote the first edition of this book I made a mistake in emphasizing the no-step at the expense of the one-step version. I may have been influenced by having stiff skis, which make the one-step double-pole a bit more difficult. In fact, since then I have come up with one small measure for determining the stiffness of skis, and that is being able to do a one-step double-pole with ease. If I get a pair of skis that make the one-step difficult, I know they are too stiff for me.

Aside from this factor, a racer must have both double-pole motions in his arsenal. Coaches are wise to teach both methods and should refrain from criticizing the use of either double-poling motion without paying attention to the following: The no-step double-pole is best used in fairly fast conditions. It is very difficult to use a long, sweeping motion with the arms when the going is fast: You simply go by your poles too fast. So shorter, more frequent poling motions are used. The hands often reach back only as far as the hips

and then swing up, fairly close in front of the face.

If the conditions are slower, the one-step double-pole is more useful than the no-step. The extension of the legs in this movement allows for a more sweeping, powerful motion of the arms (as opposite, of Braa executing the one-step). The one-step poling tempo is not so high either, but the strokes are more powerful, and the added power gained by using the legs is very significant as well. Studies have shown the one-step double-pole to be more efficient than the no-step or the diagonal stride in certain conditions.

The One-step

An excellent way for beginners to learn to ski is by swinging both arms forward along with one leg. Reaching forward with the arms seems natural to almost everyone, but driving that leg forward is not always so easy. But the same leg-drive I talk about in the diagonal is important here in the one-step double-pole. The poles are planted in the snow at the proper angle and the skier leans down on them, pushes, and away he goes. It's kind of a thrill for a person who is on skis for the first time.

The practiced racer does the same thing, but is more vigorous and quick about it. He often swoops out with both arms and gets so far forward over his skis that only putting both poles into the snow keeps him from tipping over. The forward drive is helped along by one leg—either one—that drives ahead too. The practiced racer also kicks with his rear leg as part of this one-step double-pole. The kick to the rear by one leg and the forward movement of the other leg occurs simultaneously and it's almost like a scissors action—just as in the diagonal.

You should learn to lead with either leg. Often you will be in a situation where the track dictates that you must lead with a particular leg, as in approaching a corner. Or sometimes one ski will be a bit more slippery than the other and you might prefer to lead with that one continually, while kicking with the less slippery ski.

I'm not going to dwell too much on the details of the double-pole but I will make a few more general statements.

Summarizing the one-step double-pole, in a fast track it's possible to ski at optimum speed without putting full power into each stroke, as

58. Stages in the one-step double-pole. Not all skiers use a hand-carry so high as his—but of course it's an individual matter (and with a champion skier like this, remember the old saying: "If it works, don't fix it").

in the diagonal. In fact, you might help wear yourself out by extra-vigorous poling motions when they wouldn't be really contributing to your progress along the track. This is a situation where it helps if you know the optimum effort and speed that is called for in a particular situation.

If the poles are pushed 'way out behind, and even up into the air slightly, it is probably a mistake.

First, the last part of a real long backward thrust may not give you that much extra power.

More important, however, is that all this takes time. The tempo of the double-pole, as in the diagonal, is controlled by the arms. It might be faster, and easier, to pole less vigorously and more often. In this situation you should cut off the power push of the arms right beside your body.

The No-step

With the new fiberglass skis the no-step double-pole has become increasingly important. These skis are so fast that in many situations it is a bit awkward to use even the one-step double-pole.

Almost everything I've said about poling in the one-step double-pole applies to the no-step double-pole. And be sure not to get hung up by using an extra long poling motion.

One of the key things here, as in the one-step, is to get your body weight into the poling motion. You've practiced this on roller skis and you should remember that technique. Pole and use your arms for some power until your hands are about level with your hips, then really lean on the poles with your upper body. You'll be surprised at

---

Be Sure He's a Friend, Though

There is probably nothing in the world more infuriating to an x-c skier than having someone skiing behind him who's continually clicking on the heels of his skis. So always arrange to ski behind him first, and don't keep it up too long.

In competition it can be a really dirty trick. In the 1972 Olympic relays in Sapporo I was dismayed to see one skier come into the stadium and ski more than one-half a kilometer right on the heels of the man in front of him. He wasn't just clicking the leader's heels, either: he was riding on the man's skis by a foot or more—so much that it made difficult striding for the front-runner. I'm surprised that the lead skier didn't turn around and whale him one.

some of the body positions that show up in a series of photos taken of double-poling, but these awkward-looking positions are usually a result of good technique, i.e., getting your weight into the poling motion.

Double-pole Tempo

One good way to test for the best tempo in any double-pole is to stage a few races with other skiers on parallel tracks. Or go behind one skier and use a different tempo from his and see if you can keep up with him. You will find often that the faster tempo, accompanied by a less vigorous push, will stand you in good stead.

When slower tempos are called for there is a little weight-shift you can use which is fun. At the end of the poling stroke, as you are straightening up again, raise your hands high, elbows bent, and rock your weight back slightly onto your heels. This should produce a slight planing effect and will help speed you up, or at least maintain your speed for a longer time. This shifting of the weight should be used as part of a thrust along the track and must follow soon after the poling. And you can't lean back too far or else you won't be in a good position to take another double-pole.

17. Technique for Uphill

After a lot of discussion about flat techniques it's time to face the facts. In a race, the uphills are where it's at. Studies made by the Finns, the Swiss, and even the Putney Ski Club, have shown that racers spend more time on uphills during a race than everywhere else combined. Furthermore, the differences in individual times on uphill sections account for an overwhelming percentage of the differences in times in the final results.

Probably the most important message I can give to a racer is that he must focus on uphills. This focus must include training, consideration of ski stiffness and waxing, and constant practice of techniques.

It's a bit too simplified to talk about one flat technique and one uphill technique. Excluding the double-pole, we might find some agreement for just one flat technique with slight modifications to fit snow conditions, but no experienced skier will ever admit to having only one uphill technique.

Before Choosing a Method

Before I explain some uphill techniques I will list the important variables to consider when attacking the hills during a race.

1. *Steepness.* Clearly, the slope of the hill is important. In some instances you might be forced to herringbone; in others you might be able to double-pole. There are all sorts of shades between these two extremes.

2. *Length.* If the hill is very short, with a good recovery section after it, you will want to get over the hill in the fastest possible manner, even to the point of thrashing a bit. On the other hand if the hill is long, you will need to pace yourself by using different techniques as well as by varying your speed.

3. *Your state of conditioning.* If you are in good shape and very strong, you will be able to use more of the different techniques than someone who is not so fortunate (i.e., out of shape).

4. *The wax.* Naturally, your wax will be a factor in the techniques you use. You might have no choice and be forced to herringbone every hill. Heaven forbid!

5. *The point in the race.* If you are near the end of a race you may want to take a chance on going under, because the extra time you might save by going as fast as possible is worth the risk. At any other point in the race you must be sure not to go under on a hill, no matter what technique you use.

For flat hills: the diagonal

On flat uphills most good skiers use the diagonal—the same technique that is used on the flats. This has already been covered and after a good season on the roller skis—the uphills, remember?—you will be better equipped for skiing a strong diagonal on the hills.

You should concentrate on getting some glide with each stride. If you can glide, then see if you can get about 6–8 cm more with each stride. It helps if you maintain a slightly lower body position and concentrate on the forward leg-drive with just a little hip thrust at the end of the forward leg-drive. Using the hips consciously this way is O.K., as long as you do it at the correct time. The danger is that some skiers use the hip to initiate a kicking action, forward or backward, and this is a mistake. The correct time for any hip action, again, is at the *end* of the stride. The foot penduls through, the knee drives ahead, the upper leg gets into the act with some thrust, and then the hip polishes it off.

Generally, using the diagonal on flat uphills is a very businesslike procedure. You need a strong forward drive and a strong arm push; there's no time for change-ups, or you'll lose your momentum. You must concentrate on the track and be aware of any little bumps, ripples or kickholes made by preceding skiers. These kickholes offer you a platform to spring off from, and you have to take these as they come, in rhythm. In good competition, under certain snow conditions, the kickholes in the track are pronounced. Woe to the skier who cannot use them! If he doesn't, it's almost like the difference between climbing stairs in the normal way by stepping on the treads, and trying to go up by stepping on the risers.

Some skiers have trouble knowing when to shift over to another technique. The time varies with each skier of course, but if you are having a hard time maintaining the diagonal, or your glide has stopped, or you are getting stiff and tired, it's probably time to change. The key is usually that you are not getting any glide in each stride. Under these conditions most of your forward leg-drive is going to no avail.

The double-pole also can be used under fast conditions on flat uphills, and I won't say any more than this —it's very fast and a good technique to have in your repertory. It's not too tiring when done under the right conditions.

For Steeper Hills

Well, here we are. This is where it's at. The racer who wants to finish at the top of the result list must be strong on these uphills. There's no way around it. A lot of time is spent on these hills and this is where the separations are made.

I'll mention three different techniques for attacking the steeper hills. All require a high degree of conditioning, and require that you keep your momentum, and all require skis waxed well.

Almost Running

First, imagine having snowshoes on, or short GLM skis, instead of the longer x-c skis. Thus equipped, how would you run up the hill? Actually I answered the question for you, since you would probably use motions very similar to those used in running on foot. The body would be fairly upright; you would land fairly hard on each foot or at least push off fairly hard on each foot. And you'd go just like that.

That's about the best way to describe this running technique, which is used by most of the top racers now. It's nothing beautiful to look at, it isn't too graceful. But it's powerful, fast, and therefore effective. The ski is pushed down into the track, thus setting the wax. The

59 (near frames) **& 60** (middle strip) **& 61** (frames far right). For these three vertical sequences I asked the skiers to start off on the right ski and use the diagonal to take this flat (gradual) uphill at moderate speed. No frame taken by my motor-drive camera has been omitted: to look for any differences in technique would be sheer nitpicking.

All-star line-up of world's top skiers in action during the 1979 season. Left strip, from top, **62–65:** Lars-Erik Eriksen of Norway, Maurilio DeZolt of Italy, Bill Koch of the U.S.A., Matti Pitkanen of Finland—racing in the first World Cup Race at Telemark, Wisconsin, at the start of the season in December 1978.

Middle strip, from top, **66–69:** Doug Gudwer of Canada, Juha Mieto of Finland, Oddvar Braa of Norway, Joseph Luszczek of Poland—near the beginning of the pre-Games 30-km race at Lake Placid during February 1979.

Far strip, from top, **70–73:** Sergey Saveliev of the U.S.S.R., Thomas Wassberg of Sweden, Yeygeniy Belyayev of the U.S.S.R., Oddvar Braa of Norway—on the first hill of the 15-km course at the pre-Games at Lake Placid in February 1979.

Coaches and students of x–c are continually studying the various elements of the sport, and during the past years a few of these people have focused on uphill skiing, coming up with an interesting theory. Allowing for average or natural strength differences, the argument goes on to invoke certain laws of physics and the like, concluding that a lighter person has mechanical advantages over a heavier person in climbing hills, and therefore can go up faster. I'm not so sure about this, and based on my own observations herewith offer a Caldwell Conjecture: Strength is an overriding factor in climbing hills, and a strong, big person with good technique has an advantage over a strong, smaller person with good technique.

None of the racers pictured here is what you might call the spindly type. And would you believe that Juha Mieto (**67**, middle strip) is nearly 2 meters tall and weighs about 100 kg? He too holds his own on the uphills.

62

63

64

65

arms are used for some push but also as stabilizers to a degree. This is because the running motion is a bit rough and some skiers sway from side to side slightly in anchoring the ski or setting the wax. Thus the poles keep the skier from tipping too far to the side.

The Shuffle

The latest technique being used by many top U.S. racers is the shuffle. We have worked especially hard on this one in our area during the past few years.

The shuffle is best adapted for powder-snow conditions and the following features typify this technique: The forward-sliding, or shuffling, of the leg is marked. There is not much kick or lifting of the rear ski off the snow. The body position is farther back than in other techniques. The arms are not used powerfully; in fact, with a high leg tempo the arms cannot keep up the pace and sometimes are out of rhythm, or syncopated.

The advantages of the shuffle are very simple, yet so important. First, the body weight is not hoisted up so far as in other techniques. Even if the difference in the lift is only a few cm, think of the extra work, or energy, that you can save over the span of a race!

Next, the more you practice the shuffle, the more easily you will develop a very high tempo. And high tempos always go with fast times.

Several of the Swedes use this technique, most notably Sven–Ake Lundbeck. He looks bowlegged and awkward in doing so, but you can't fault gold medals.

Some skiers actually find that a combination run-and-shuffle works well for them. Whether this is due to their particular strengths and body builds, their wax, or their skis' stiffness is not so important as the fact that the technique is fast and relaxed. We have dubbed this the "ruffle."

Hill-bounding Again

Another method for climbing is one very similar to the hill-bounding exercise prescribed for dry-land training. In hill-bounding, during each stride or bound you keep your momentum going and it carries you forward onto the lead ski. You set your wax and almost simultaneously bound to the next ski. This takes a great deal of finesse in keeping the ski flat (or placing it where it won't be so likely to slip—such as a section of track that is less steep than surrounding sections), and using a lot of forward ankle-bend, which in turn means having rubber-like knees and ankles that help you to use a lot of flexion, thus cushioning each bound.

You must think about coming off the ball of each foot with each step.

166

Ski-bounding

Don't think about such things as getting the foot forward, or kicking back, or sneaking through the woods like an Indian, and so on: these ideas are likely to lead to faulty technique. Keep your weight forward, keep your feet so close to being under you that you don't have to struggle to get into the position where you set the wax and spring off with the next step.

One of the worst things you can do is slide or kick your foot forward and weight the heel of the ski, for then you have to overcome gravity in order to be able to get into the position where you can slide the other foot forward so you can weight your heel and then have to overcome gravity in order to——I'm getting tired. How about you?

The length of the bound depends on the steepness of the hill and your own strength and build. On very steep hills where you can bound, the length is necessarily shortened. But if you are in good shape the bound will actually take you farther than sliding the ski forward would do. This extra distance comes from the spring and the forward-rolling motion of the body. In fact, some of the real brutes bound and have enough power to get a short glide,

74. This sequence shows how a racer can use body-build, conditioning, good technique and concentration to best advantage.

even on some of the steep uphills.

Your arms of course are very useful, but you should not depend on them too much for power in this stride. If you do, you will slow up and get tired, both at the same time. Your legs are the tools to use in getting uphill. If you need a lot of help from the arms your wax probably isn't good enough, and you should switch techniques. However, it's fine to use the arms as an aid to balance, for a little extra push at the right time, and to prevent serious backsliding. Remember that the arms are not, and never will be, the primary propelling force for getting up any hill most economically.

The differences between this good bounding technique and bulling it are a matter of body motion. In hill-bounding there is more knee and ankle flexion, the tempo is a bit slower, each stride is longer since you attempt to bound forward more, and it's smoother-looking. In comparison the running technique might be illustrated this way 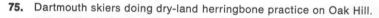 and hill-bounding this way and the shuffle this way.

CPTK 5: In hill-climbing, above all get maximum use from your legs.

The dogtrot

I dubbed this method in an earlier book and it's still a pretty good way

75. Dartmouth skiers doing dry-land herringbone practice on Oak Hill.

for getting up steep hills. The dog-trot is not as fast as running or ski-bounding and therefore it's easier. It's a nice step to use when you're tired. (I don't really want to call it an old person's technique since I have been guilty of using it in races all my life.)

Dogtrotting is almost like ski-bounding, but with two vital differences. First, the length of each stride is shorter, hence my calling it a trot. Second, there is no emphasis on springing off the ball of the foot and straightening the leg underneath while moving forward and upward. Instead, you almost fall forward off the ball of the lead foot and save yourself from tipping over into the snow by getting the other foot ahead. These important differences make for a pretty relaxed technique.

The body position is the same as that in ski-bounding; also the same is the idea of keeping your feet under you and not being forced to overcome gravity by getting the lead foot too far ahead. The poling action in a dogtrot need not be quite so vigorous as in ski-bounding, and it's also easier to use a lot of change-ups.

The herringbone

I must confess that I never have been too swift at the herringbone, but I have seen a lot of skiers who find this method very relaxing.

They'll break into a herringbone while others are still ski-bounding. There's no question of the importance of the herringbone and it should be practiced on dry land every chance you get. Running up sandbanks or gravel pits offers possibilities for such practice.

The important point in the herringbone is again to use the legs and not to concentrate too much on the use of the poles and arms. In fact, sometimes you're likely to get all fouled up with your poles getting in the way; some skiers will just lift their poles and bull it up the hill with the herringbone.

Using the legs will require edging the skis enough to keep them from slipping, and this in turn requires a certain amount of flexibility. One of the most common errors is to take steps that are too long, or to bend too much at the waist. In this extreme forward position you are not pushing with your skis against the hill so much, but rather against the top layer of snow. In this case you're likely to slip since the snow on hills that require the herringbone is always beat-up and softer than in other sections of the track.

So stay as upright as you can, take shorter steps rather than longer ones, and then begin to work on your tempo. The difference in tempos is absolutely startling. Some skiers look like human eggbeaters going up hills with the herringbone, and others (me?) look like old cows.

Getting it all together

Assuming you have all these techniques at your disposal, you still have to decide which ones to use. In a race on a long hill I would suggest that you begin conservatively, even using the dogtrot as a warm-up. (It's better to cool it at the bottom of a long hill and come off the top like a jet rather than really to fire in at the bottom and crump out at the top.) Then, after getting the feel of the situation, you might start a more aggressive diagonal, or some running or ski-bounding.

Vary your techniques with the terrain and according to how you feel. Be sure to exhale and inhale deeply all the time—use change-ups and different techniques as a method of relaxation. Keep the top of the hill in your mind, and then ski fast off the top—toward the next downhill.

Conjecture: On a fairly long hill of constant grade, there may be a significant cardiovascular advantage to be gained by switching techniques occasionally.

I have no firm evidence for this, and it will take a long time to prove or disprove it, but try it sometime. Attack the hill and, when you begin to get those warning signals indicating you might go under, switch your technique. I don't mean to pull up and slow down to a walk, but instead to keep up your same speed, insofar as you can judge, and use a different method. For instance, if you'd been using a modified running technique to the point where you began to stiffen slightly, shift over to a shuffle.

The main idea is to put stress on different muscles by changing your body position.

18. Technique for Downhill

There has been a lot of focus on downhill skiing techniques and downhill waxing for x-c racing during the last few years. To be sure, these items are important, and in the big leagues every difference makes a difference. But there has been undue emphasis on speed waxing for downhills at the expense of the climbing wax for uphills, and in many cases this has resulted in weaker race results.

The studies I referred to at the start of Chapter 17 have shown rather conclusively that there is little or no correlation between the top finishers and the racers who were fastest on the downhill sections in any given race. In fact, one might conclude that some of the slower skiers on the downhill sections compensated by doing the best ultimately.

After you get your flat and uphill techniques nailed down, go to work on your downhills. And even though your downhill technique may be the least important of the three, you can be sure that you will never be a champion unless it is fairly solid.

But First the Variables

There are several factors that help determine your speed down a hill and they are fairly easy to understand.

Because of their design, some skis are just plain faster than others. Often the skis with soft tips go faster, and this is because the tips bend easily to conform better with the small bumps or ripples in the track. Narrower skis are usually faster too.

The wax and the ski bottoms also make a difference.

But if all these factors are equal, have you ever noticed that another fellow can always beat you on a downhill? Even if you swear it's the skis and you switch with him, he beats you again. Well, he sure can ski downhill better than you, and that's all there is to it. He probably steers his skis ever so carefully, making sure the tips do not dig into the edge of the track. He probably rides back on his skis occasionally. If he is standing straight up he weights his heels, if he crouches he presents less wind resistance and again weights the tails of his skis. He probably unweights, or rides up over bumps, better than you. And so on.

The whole idea is to present as little friction as possible between the

76. A rock-steady tuck is just about perfect form for straight downhill sections.

skis and the snow, and to present a minimum of wind resistance. The planing effect gained by leaning back is a help. Clearly, unweighting over bumps and not hitting the edge of the track with ski tips also helps. These are all fine distinctions, but they separate the skiers.

What to do

The most important thing you can do during a race is to relax on the downhills. If holding a crouch is going to tire you, forget it. Stand up and lean back, weighting the rear of your skis, and relax. Or lean over slightly and rest your forearms on your legs, just above the knees. This will cut wind resistance a little and is very restful.

If you have the training—the technique plus the conditioning—then go ahead and try to ride a flat ski. Don't edge any more than necessary; lean back, crouch, and steer your turns holding that crouch, especially at slower speeds where straightening up would present a lot of wind resistance; and

172

ride the bumps by unweighting or flexing the legs (knees). On good straight tracks you can even let your head drop for short sections until your nose is pointing down toward the track: this cuts wind resistance and is more restful than holding your head up to look at what is ahead.

On fast winding downhills, you must possess good Alpine ability and treat your skis just as you would Alpine skis. The newest fiberglass x-c skis, particularly those made by some of the world's leading Alpine ski manufacturers like Fischer, behave very much like Alpine skis and you can carve good fast turns with them. In rough terrain they follow the track

---

Grand Prix Stuff

In Sapporo during the 1972 Olympics many of the coaches checked their wax before every race on a section of track near the start. This section had a steep downhill followed by a long flat and we often went out there and took turns skiing down to see how far out on the flat we could coast: the farther we coasted, the better the wax.

A bunch of coaches from one country would usually go in succession. Each would coast to a stop, hop out of the track, make his mark, and wait to see where his countrymen would stop, invariably they would all stand around for a few minutes after their test and discuss the wax. At this point our staff would boom down. I happened to have a particularly fast pair of skis with good bottoms and soft tips. I always waxed that pair with the fastest wax I knew of for the particular snow condition that day and when I skied down the hill I rocked back on my heels so far and so hard that my toes were practically sticking up through the tops of my boots. I held my downhill tuck until my legs burned. In addition, the track had a little left skate turn at the bottom—and if there is one turn I can do (even in a tuck) this happens to be it—the skate turn to the left.

Weighing more than the average coach, I guess I had about all the advantages possible on a well-packed track, so it's no wonder that I invariably won the International Wax Race. Of course I made the best of it, coasting by the other coaches and shaking my head at them in disbelief, or chortling ever so slightly, or just acting as if this were the way it always was.

very well too, if you either steer them or use the whole ski to make a turn.

It may seem paradoxical that I am stressing Alpine skiing right here instead of the step turn, the skate turn and even the Telemark turn—that most elegant maneuver unique to x-c. These turns are the hallmarks of touring technique, which in today's racing you just don't have time for. Alpine methods have superseded these classics in top-level racing.

No matter what else you do on downhills, breathe deeply. Exhale as much as you can—force everything out, then inhale slowly and deeply. In addition to getting more O_2 into your system this may also help relax you.

19. Technique for Poor Tracks

At the U.S. Nationals in 1979 there were two days of racing when the air temperature was creeping up over the freezing mark and the snow temperature was getting close to freezing. If it had been klister snow it would have been just another day, but instead it was powder and the tracks started to glaze and get wobbly and the waxing was difficult. Many people missed the wax, some racers stopped to re-wax during the race, and others just slugged it out. Most observers cited the conditions as being "tough" but this is a factor that the bare results do not show. There's no special category in the result list for those who missed the wax, or weren't used to skiing in glazed conditions, or just plain didn't like the track.

Many skiers and coaches expect too much too often in the way of tracks, and since we have swung around nearly full circle on the business of track-setting, I think that it's time for a slightly different approach.

When I began skiing x-c about 1942 we used to practice in loose snow until enough of us had produced a track with our skis. That track, at best, was pretty wobbly. On race days we looked forward to being able to ski in a better track, one prepared by the same method but with greater care.

It wasn't long before we all sensed a need for pole tracks, and so the organizers of the better races used to make four parallel tracks in the snow. We used the middle two tracks for our skis and the outside two for the poles. This was a big advance! At about the same time we all got the idea of having snowshoers, or skiers sidestepping the course, to pack the snow—and this was great. The only problem was to get the tracks in before the snow froze solid.

As late as 1966 the Norwegians, who were running the FIS championships, employed their army to work on the courses. A few hundred soldiers were on the course every day, shoveling snow, sidestepping the courses, and putting in tracks "by hand." Meanwhile in this country we had already switched to mechanical snowpacking devices and track sleds.

From about 1966 on, our x-c skiers have come more and more to depend on good tracks for racing and for practice. Coaches continually exclaim that you can't practice ski-racing techniques and tempos unless you have a good, fast, hard-packed track, just like the ones you will be racing on. Well, that's mostly correct—but at the same time I think we have gone too far: our skiers are spoiled by too many good tracks and are losing out in several respects.

For one thing, I don't care where the race is, you don't always get a good track. Anyone who has been in competition long enough knows that. So there is an advantage in being something of a mudder. And you don't develop a mudder's ability by staying in good tracks all the time.

For another, many skiers are losing training opportunities because "the tracks aren't set" or "the snowmobile broke down." This is ridiculous, of course. If you are interested in being a good competitor you should get out to train under all conditions.

I was most impressed with Oddvar Braa and Magne Myrmo, two of Norway's leading skiers who visited me during their stay in the States in February of 1973. We had just been blessed with an eight-inch, wet-powder snowstorm. It was the Norwegians' last day in Putney and they wanted to practice before leaving at noon for a race that evening, but we didn't have time to set any tracks. However, some boys were working on one of our trails, getting it ready for an upcoming race, and they had gone out into the woods on a snowmobile for a couple of kilometers. The Norwegians put on some yellow klister, the only wax that would work that day, went out and skied back and forth on the snowmobile tracks for about 30 km, then came back in smiling and happy. Excellent workout, they said. I thought of the number of U.S. skiers who wouldn't have skied that day, either because there were no tracks, or because the waxing conditions were tough.

Further, by skiing in tracks that aren't perfect, having little quirks and bumps or soft spots, you will develop better balance and a kind of strength that isn't developed by skiing in those deep, hard, good, straight tracks.

Perhaps I can draw a parallel between weight-lifting and logging. You can lift weights, using all the proper techniques and safeguards, and develop all sorts of strength for lifting those weights. But this conditioning doesn't necessarily train you to stand on a sidehill with a chainsaw trying to limb a tree, or to stand with one foot perched up on a stump trying to throw four-foot chunks of wood over a windfall or a pile of brush you have just cut.

Still more: skiing in some loose snow, or on crust, can help develop good technique and strength. I've skied with people my own weight on light crust and watched them sink through because of the way they kicked—too hard and all at once. I've seen lots of skiers who couldn't set their wax even in the loose snow that sometimes accumulates in a good race track during a snowstorm. And by skiing through a little snow you can get marvelous strength and balance training for your stride.

And finally, skiing without tracks is a nice diversion. Usually it's one pack of fun. That's the way this x-c stuff started, after all.

77. In a seemingly unhurried atmosphere for a pre-race scene, skiers and officials relax before the start of the New South Wales Championships, winter of 1977. (See photo 53, page 145, for comments on a snow condition not unusual for Australia.)

20. General Summary

"PI" has meant many things to me during my time in Putney. First I associated it with poison ivy, which I am very susceptible to. I once told my doctor, when requesting some preventive shots for the stuff, that I got it on the soles of my feet when I skied over PI patches in the winter.

Next, PI is the abbreviation we use for the Putney Inn, one of the local watering spots.

And not long ago I began using the initials to stand for Primary Importance. I rank PI items on a descending scale of 1 to 3 right now, and mentally I categorize the things I hear some of the coaches and racers talk about. I think we all need to grade such items and behave accordingly.

For instance, I consider training and technique PI–1 items. I hope there is no disagreement.

I consider the color of your socks, the length of the poles to the nearest ½ cm, the kind of heel-plate you use, the number of klister skis you have (in excess of one), and a whole raft of other things as PI–3 items. They really are not items to get hung up on.

A good example of a PI–2 item is the stiffness of your skis; this can make a big difference. Another PI–2 would be the kicker-wax you are using. Since I consider the Alpine wax used for downhills less important than the kicker-wax, it ranks a 3 with me (though I'd really like to rank it 2.5).

For Coaches: Part of the Challenge

The human body is like a finely tuned engine, and each body, like each engine, is slightly different. I liken different bodies to the five different combustion engines I count on at home in Vermont while gardening, mowing lawns, tapping maple trees at the start of sugaring, or cutting firewood. Each of the engines works well, but each takes a different gasoline mixture, a different starting procedure, and different treatment for optimum results. If I treated my chainsaw like my powered tapper I probably wouldn't get much wood cut. And so if we expect optimum results from different people we must not try to treat them all alike.

The main point is not to get continually thrown by PI–3 items. If they aren't just so, they probably don't matter much so long as the PI–1's and 2's are in line.

Spend most of your time trying to improve the standing of PI–1 items, then PI–2's; and finally, if you have the time and inclination, you can get really finicky about the PI–3's.

Pacing and Concentration

The matters of pacing and concentration are not focused on by enough coaches or racers in North America. In fact, I see an almost opposite effect caused by many coaches exhorting their skiers to "Go for it!" or to "Punch it!" or to "Go hard!" All these encouragements probably cause the racers to tighten up, go under, or otherwise ski less than optimally.

These exhortations may have their basis in the following notion: If you come in from a race tired and exhausted, you feel you have spent your energy supply and therefore have done your best. The corollary is that if you come across the finish line feeling refreshed and relaxed, or at least as if you could go on farther, you have taken too much time, and had you gone faster earlier you would have had better results. So it follows that you should "Go for it!"

Well, this is not the way to go. Better that you come in feeling a reserve of energy. This probably means that you have been able to finish hard instead of struggling at the end. If you are struggling, tense, or actually going under on any part of the course it's surprising how much time you can lose. To see this, study some tired skiers at the end of the race. Jump in behind them and notice how slowly they are going. I've even finished races, relaxed a bit, and gone out to test this myself. (The first time I did this I chuckled to myself to note how slowly one of my competitors was going. Then I found out that his time beat mine, which showed—for one thing—that my pacing was worse than his.)

So it's better to build a base of confidence: feeling good at the finish and knowing you can go faster next time out—rather than worrying about having gone too fast, and knowing that next time you must slow down somewhere if you are going to have a needed reserve. Skiing optimally, therefore, requires pacing. And pacing means more than skiing as fast as possible without going under. With some skiers this intense pace may not be feasible, or may pose too great a risk. Correct pacing is difficult to define, or prescribe, since it varies with the racer. But examples of pacing abound, particularly in the longer races. Thomas Wassberg, the Swedish star, is famous for his rather slow starts and his blistering finishes. He manages quite well in world competition too.

Check the lap times for a 50-km race and you will always find the winners have kept the best pace and the also-rans have fallen off, or started too fast.

Pacing is not a naturally occurring phenomenon used by all racers. Instead, it is a very conscious and disciplined part of ski racing. It is the most individual aspect of racing and you must practice it to become familiar with your capabilities.

In order to learn about pacing, or how fast you can go in different terrain, it's necessary to practice and feel it out during training. I know some skiers who can go all out on flat sections of courses, yet who must pace themselves on uphills. Others feel it necessary to pace themselves on downhills, not working so hard to hold a deep crouch, because this tires them too much. It's a truly individual situation.

Perhaps you can get an idea for pacing by listening to, or feeling, your heart rate. Perhaps you will learn to recognize the warning signals just before you go under, and to let these indicators tell you to slow down.

It's always a good idea to ski behind someone who is thrashing or generally tight in order to realize how easy it is for you to go as fast in a relaxed manner. You must be able to ski like this when you are alone on the race course.

Once you begin the race it is very important to set a proper pace. Here is a place where a coach can really help. If he can give you your time in relation to the other skiers at about the 1-km point you will get a good notion of how your pace is going. If you are going to be competitive you will have to be within a reasonable time of the faster skiers at this point. On the other hand, if you are several seconds ahead of everyone it may mean you are starting too fast.

At the pre-Olympic Games 30-km race at Lake Placid in 1979 I was checking times on all racers at 1-km for my information. One American, a notoriously fast starter who often burns out later, was a full 7 seconds ahead of the field. This was clearly too fast and I called out to tell him so. He heard me, and reduced almost to a touring speed, by comparison with his previous rate. But he went on to run a good race, and no doubt this information he received early in the going helped him to make a better over-all showing than if he'd become tight and exhausted later on the course.

It helps to have lots of "starts" or timed workouts during training just to get used to the idea of being under the clock. Maybe you won't get seized up when the real winter races come along.

In sum: The whole point is to be able to ski at the necessary high speed in a relaxed manner without going under, or without feeling you are tightening up.

For Coaches: Dealing with the Press

Press coverage is wonderful, just the sort of "PR" that most promoters of x-c have been striving for over the years. But coverage of individuals must be watched, and this is a job for the coach.

At top-level races the organizers often schedule a press conference for the medal winners after the race, when the athletes have had a chance to shower and rest up a bit. This is a very proper occasion and should be encouraged. I'll admit that the occasional international coach whisks his athletes off after a race and they are not seen by anyone until the next day, at the earliest; but this is not common practice. The press conference really is a command performance and it is clearly in an athlete's best interest to attend. If he doesn't, he is likely to be pestered at all hours during the next few days by inquiring reporters.

If an athlete attends the conference he should not feel obliged to give other interviews afterward. From then on, it should be his own free choice.

At lower-level races, especially those not accorded formal conferences, most athletes feel flattered at being interviewed and are very obliging. If the coach feels his athletes are in jeopardy of getting more tired and run down, he should try to co-ordinate these activities to everyone's best interest.

At the kids' level, PR is good again, but the same warnings obtain.

Over-all, the coach best knows each athlete and should try to help with the publicity so it will not adversely affect his skiers. The written word has a big impact and reporters who do not understand the sport, or are looking for sensational stories which will sell, can hinder a skier's future.

Concentration

Just before the start of a race you should be going over your race strategy. This might simply be a rehash of a plan arrived at earlier, perhaps the day before when you studied the course. The plan must be based on your conditioning and your confidence to ski the course. Banter and last-minute talk before the start might interrupt your concentration.

After you start and establish what you consider is a good pace it's not simply a matter of skiing in to the finish. You will have to concentrate on the corners, trying to save seconds, or fractions thereof, on them. Parts of the track may vary and you must use the best technique for these sections too; faced with two tracks, you must choose the faster.

And all the while you must be conscious of the signals from your body. Can you go a little faster? Or should you slow a bit?

Veteran racers also get a feel for the snow and know when they are using the best technique and the optimum effort for the conditions. It does no good to exert yourself in order to get a good glide in slow snow conditions. Yet some skiers don't vary their techniques to offset differences in the snow.

There are human distractions to deal with too. Crowd encouragement is usually helpful, but I've known plenty of racers to get carried away by the cheers and simply go under on the next hill.

Daydreaming is another way not to go. You must continually be aware of where you are on the course. If a few hundred meters of track pass by without conscious recognition of them you probably aren't working well enough on the business at hand.

And feeling sorry for yourself is often the signal of potentially poor results. You not only lose your concentration, but you defeat yourself as well.

Extremes of Cold

The FIS X–C Committee has begun a discussion of how to deal with very cold temperatures during a meet, and eventually this will lead to the establishment of some rules. Nothing has been decided at this writing, but the problem certainly came to a head during the pre-Olympic Games meet at Lake Placid and the World Junior Championships in Quebec in February 1979. That winter the eastern part of North America experienced record cold weather, and most of it came during these two big meets.

At Lake Placid, Juha Mieto, the giant Finn, suffered a frost-bitten stomach in the 15-k race as he came in on the last 5 k's, which are predominantly downhill. (Perhaps he should have stayed longer in a tuck.) Other racers froze their ears, cheeks, fingers, and toes; some were even forced to quit. Meanwhile the Russians, who are accustomed to these temperatures around −20° Celsius (−5° Fahrenheit), raced barehanded!

During meetings of the team leaders at Placid and subsequently at Quebec, it was clear from listening that what's cold for the French, or the Italians, is just a normal day for the Scandinavians and is probably regarded as a heat wave by the Russians.

Later that spring Mike Brady, my friend and noted x-c author, and I were discussing how to handle this problem of cold, and he told me that at a meeting of coaches from Scandinavia and Russia a very interesting thing happened. Each country had been asked to name a minimum temperature for racing. The Norwegians came in with the warmest temperature, the Swedes had the next warmest, the Finns the next, and the Russians the coldest temperature. The colder the country, the colder the temperature. So it looks like a skier's tolerance for cold is a matter of regional conditioning.

I assume the FIS committee will take this factor into account and establish a fairly comfortable temperature as a minimum. If it gets too warm for the Russians, say around −15 C, perhaps they can race in shorts and T−shirts.

Some tips for dealing with cold

I've seen a fair number of cold weather routines and some of these may help you, or your racers.

Clothing

Long underwear is taken for granted in cold weather. Some racers use it every race as a matter of course. Some underwear, like Lifa, wicks the perspiration very well and gives the wearer a feeling of comfort.

Headgear should be warm and able to absorb a large amount of sweat. Some racers wear earbands over or under their regular hats, and then rotate both slightly during the race to bring a drier portion over their foreheads. Other skiers actually change to dry hats during a race. Still others wear special bands across their foreheads to help prevent the sweat from getting into their eyes.

The boots are lighter and colder than ever and therefore many racers are forced to use regular socks, or special slipper-like affairs which fit over the boots and keep the feet warmer.

Once your feet and head are warm, you are in pretty good shape—assuming you have long johns on and a good suit over them. With warm head and feet, you may be surprised to find how easy it is to keep your hands warm. (Those Russians aren't so tough—it's just that their feet and heads are well taken care of.)

Many racers warm up with heavy gloves until their hands are nearly sweating, then switch to lighter racing gloves. Skiers with tougher hands warm up with the light gloves until they are warm, and then race bare-handed. I have found that if I warm up properly and wear enough clothing, as described above, I can ski comfortably without gloves at −10 C. But each skier will have his own preference and will have to experiment.

Some new racing suits have windbreaker material built in to their fronts and normal stretch material for the rest. These are very good in cold weather, or on courses with long downhill sections.

Factors to Watch

Many racers cover their faces with Vaseline to protect against frostbite, or wind-chill.

Naturally, most of us are alert to wind-chill during windy weather. But remember, even if the wind isn't blowing, when you get going on fast downhills you create your own wind-chill. This is no doubt what did in Mieto at Lake Placid in '79.

The humidity makes a difference too. There is "dry cold" and "wet cold," and that wet cold can really get to you.

So it's not simply a matter of reading the thermometer. Pay attention to wind-chill produced by nature on the skier, and the humidity.

Finally, if a racer complains of being cold during a race, coaches must not be afraid to pull him right off the course. Not many race finishes I can think of are worth frozen fingers and toes.

And Then, the Immeasurables

When all is said and done you might wonder exactly what constitutes the best program for developing x-c racers. Is it a combination of good coaching at schools or training academies, with top performers benefiting from built-in incentive programs that include free plane tickets, uniforms, room and board, and lots of equipment? Sounds great. But there is no clear answer to this question: otherwise everyone would be turning out top racers.

As I look around the world at all the different approaches I do see certain numbers of constants, or givens, surfacing. Since we seem to be at the crossroads in development here in North America, it is very important to take note of these factors.

No doubt having good coaching available is important. Attendance at a skiing school, whether it is public or private, will help. Going to a racing academy will help too, although they are still so new that it's impossible to make a long-range judgment from here.

Incentive programs are a positive factor too. Skiers who get rewarded for good performances—by being given attention in the press, transport to big races out of the area, free equipment, free lodging and meals, and all the rest—obviously provide an example worth following. Still, I can't help feeling that a lot of people and organizations who really are eager to produce good skiers are headed a bit off-course. We see a lot of skiers who have had the "treatment," the rewards and the support, quitting. Naturally dropouts are to be expected since the number of competitors has swelled so much lately. But many of the recent dropouts are quitting because they have lost the incentive benefits, mainly material benefits like those mentioned above. If a skier can no longer qualify for the traveling team, so to speak, and then quits, we have to assume that he was mainly interested in the material benefits and not so much in those immeasurables like general enjoyment of life or a feeling that he is doing the right thing.

If we were to take a good look at the top Nordic athletes in the United States at this time we would find certain things common to them. First, they come from skiing communities where competition is a normal activity. Also, they come from families who have long been supportive of ski competition. Further, until the time when they reached national prominence, few, if any, were the beneficiaries of the give-away programs we see now being developed for young skiers. In other words, they made it on their own, with the encouragement and support of their own families, and local communities, in some cases. Finally, we would find that skiing and training are as natural in their areas as the snow and the trees and the trails and the ski jumps. They have not traveled much outside their area; nor has much been contrived for them.

In short, the concept that seems to work for our best racers is similar to that which is used in the Scandinavian countries—and perhaps not very like the policy exemplified in the Eastern Bloc nations.

Simply put, there are mystical benefits that accrue from the approach that keeps them in their home area longer.

Chances are good that our top skiers will continue to come from situations I've described, where skiing and training are a natural part of their lives. It will not work to transport would-be athletes into unnatural surroundings and train them for long periods of time in the hope of producing gold medalists. There cannot be an arbitrary separation of competition and training from the basic way of life.

One of the facts we must recognize—in case we're allowed by the new breed of promoters to forget it—is this: Often many of our best skiers tell us that they will be happy if only they can do their best. Statements like this bring forth growls from certain segments of the press, from some of the high-pressure organizers and administrators, and from the general public. Their pitch is, "We don't want just your best! We want the gold medals."

While it can't be proved, I feel confident that the best we have are indeed our best because they believe that a gold, matchless thrill though it be, is not everything in life. They know the competition is fantastic, they know the realities of x-c ski racing, and they know they have really achieved something great even if they come in only second or third or wherever. They measure themselves against themselves, as well as against their competition, and want always to do their best. Is winning really confined to first place?

Index

Index